Cistercian Studies Series: Number Sixty-three

THE CHIMAERA OF HIS AGE:

STUDIES ON BERNARD OF CLAIRVAUX

CISTERCIAN STUDIES SERIES: NUMBER SIXTY-THREE

The Chimaera of His Age:
STUDIES ON BERNARD OF CLAIRVAUX

STUDIES IN MEDIEVAL CISTERCIAN HISTORY V

Edited by

E. ROZANNE ELDER

JOHN R. SOMMERFELDT

Cistercian Publications Inc.
Kalamazoo, Michigan
1980

Available in the Commonwealth and Europe from

A. R. Mowbray & Co Ltd
St Thomas House Becket Street
Oxford OX1 1SJ

TO

JEAN LECLERCQ,

monk of Clervaux,

'A Sign of Admirable

Freedom'

TABLE OF CONTENTS

Editor's Introduction
John R. Sommerfeldt
ix

General Abbreviations
xi

Abbreviations
The Works of Bernard of Clairvaux
xii

The Church as Bride in Bernard of Clairvaux's Sermons on the Song of Songs
Theresa Moritz
3

Ethical Theology in the Sermons on the Song of Songs
William O. Paulsell
12

Humanism in Bernard of Clairvaux: Beyond Literary Culture
Emero Stiegman
23

Bernardian Ideas in Wolfram's *Parzival* about Christian War and Human Development
John H. Cleland
39

The Entrance of the Cistercians into the Church Hierarchy, 1098–1227
Joel Lipkin
62

St Bernard and the Cistercian Office at the Abbey of the Paraclete
Chrysogonus Waddell OCSO
76

St Bernard and the Pagan Classics: An Historical View
Thomas Renna
122

The Appeal of Reason in St Bernard's *De diligendo Dei*
Luke Anderson OCSO
132

The Meaning of Maundy According to St Bernard
Hugh McCaffery OCSO
140

INTRODUCTION

Bernard of Clairvaux, a son of the lord of Fontaines-lès-Dijon, entered the New Monastery at Cîteaux in 1112. He brought with him some thirty companions, more than doubling the community. Only four years later, he was chosen to lead a new foundation which was called Clairvaux. Largely because of Bernard's influence, the Cistercians were to possess 343 houses all over Europe by his death in 1153.

But Bernard was not only the leader of this new wave of monastic reform, he became the leader of Europe in the first half of the twelfth century. Bernard's influence on his own time was so great that we tend to identify him with the age in which he lived, as well as identify his age with him, so that many have spoken of the 'Age of Saint Bernard.'

Thus it is no mere romanticism which has led historians with many and varied interests to study and restudy Bernard and his works. Despite the outpouring of *Festschriften*, monographs, and articles which deluged the scholarly world on the occasion of the eighth centenary of Bernard's death in 1953 and eight-hundredth anniversary of his canonization in 1974, interest in Bernard and studies of his life and thought continue on a large scale.

Most of the studies collected here were presented originally at the Seventh and Eighth Conferences on Cistercian Studies held in conjunction with the Twelfth and Thirteenth Conferences on Medieval Studies at Western Michigan University in May of 1977 and 1978. It was my pleasure to be the host at these meetings—a pleasure which evokes no little nostalgia as I contemplate the fact that—for the first time—I shall not be able to join the scholars meeting at the Tenth Conference shortly to convene. A University President's lot is not always a happy one. I am grateful to my successor as host, Rozanne Elder, who has also done the lion's share of the work on this volume.

John R. Sommerfeldt

The University of Dallas

General Abbreviations

CF   Cistercian Fathers Series. Cistercian Publications: Spencer, MA-Kalamazoo, MI. 1969-.

CS   Cistercian Studies Series. Cistercian Publications. 1969-.

MS(S)   Manuscript(s)

PG   J.-P. Migne, *Patrologiae cursus completus, series graeca*, 162 volumes. Paris, 1957-66.

PL   J.-P. Migne, *Patrologiae cursus completus, series latina*, 221 volumes. Paris, 1844-64.

RB   The Rule of St Benedict for Monasteries

SBOp   *Sancti Bernardi Opera*, edd. J. Leclercq, H. M. Rochais and C. H. Talbot. Rome, 1957-79.

ABBREVIATIONS

The Works of Bernard of Clairvaux

The works of Saint Bernard are abbreviated according to the sigla adopted by Jean Leclercq and H. M. Rochais in *Sancti Bernardi Opera* (Rome: Editiones Cistercienses, 1957–1979).

Abb	Sermo ad abbates
Abael	Epistola in erroribus Abaelardi
Adv	Sermo in adventu domini
And	Sermo in natali sancti Andreae
Ann	Sermo in annuntiatione dominica
Apo	Apologia ad Guillelmum abbatem
Asc	Sermo in ascensione Domini
Asspt	Sermo in assumptione B.V.M.
Bapt	Epistola de baptismo
Ben	Sermo in natali sancti Benedicti
Circ	Sermo in circumcisione domini
Clem	Sermo in natali sancti Clementis
Conv	Sermo de conversione ad clericos
Csi	De consideratione libri v
Ded	Sermo in dedicatione ecclesiae
Dil	Liber de diligendo deo
Div	Sermones de diversis
Epi	Sermo in epiphania domini
Ept Ma	Epitaphium sancti Malachiae
Gra	Liber de gratia et libero arbitrio
IV HM	Sermo in feria iv hebdomadae sanctae
V HM	Sermo in cena domini
Hmn Mal	Hymnus de sancto Malachiae
Hum	Liber de gradibus humilitatis et superbiae
Humb	Sermo in obitu Domni Humberti
Innoc	Sermo in festivitatibus sancti, Stephani, sancti Ioannis et sanctorum Innocentium
JB	Sermo in nativitate sancti Ioannis Baptistae
Mal	Sermo in transitu sancti Malachiae episcopi
Mart	Sermo in festivitate sancti Martini episcopi
Mich	Sermo in festo sancti Michaëlis
Miss	Hom. super missus est in laudibus Virginis Matris
Mor	Ep. de moribus et officiis episcoporum
Nat	Sermo in nativitate domini
Nat BVM	Sermo in nativitate B.V.M.
I Nov	Sermo in dominica I novembris
O Epi	Sermo in octava epiphania domini
O Asspt	Sermo dominica infra octavam assumptionis

O Pasc	Sermo in octava paschae
OS	Sermo in festivitate Omnium Sanctorum
Of Vict	Officium de sancto Victore
Palm	Sermo in ramis palmarum
Par	Parabolae
Pasc	Sermo in die Paschae
Pr Ant	Prologus in Antiphonarium
p Epi	Sermo in dominica I post octavam Epiphaniae
Pent	Sermo in die sancto pentecostes
Pl	Sermo in conversione sancti Pauli
Pre	Liber de pracepto et dispensatione
IV p P	Sermo in dominica quarta post Pentecosten
VI p P	Sermo in dominica sexta post Pentecosten
PP	Sermo in festo SS. Apostolorum Petri et Pauli
Pur	Sermo in purificatione B.V.M.
QH	Sermo super psalmum Qui habitat
Quad	Sermo in Quadragesima
Rog	Sermo in rogationibus
SC	Sermo super Cantica canticorum
I Sent	Sententiae (PL 183, 747-58)
II Sent	Sententiae (PL 184, 1135-56)
Sept	Sermo in Septuagesima
Tpl	Liber ad milites templi (De laude novae militiae)
V And	Sermo in vigilia sancti Andreae
Vict	Sermo in natali sancti Victoris
V Mal	Vita sancti Malachiae
V Nat	Sermo in vigilia nativitatis domini
V PP	Sermo in vigilia apostolorum Petri et Pauli

I am a kind of chimaera of my age, neither cleric nor
layman. I have long since stripped off the way of life,
but not the habit, of the monk. I do not wish to write
about myself what I suppose you have heard from others:
what I am doing, what I am up to, the crises in the world
I am involved in, indeed, the precipices down which I am
being cast. If you have not already heard, I would ask
you to make inquiries and, according to what you do hear,
offer your advice and the support of your prayers.

                    Bernard of Clairvaux, *Letter 250.4*

THE CHURCH AS BRIDE IN BERNARD OF CLAIRVAUX'S
SERMONS ON THE SONG OF SONGS

THERESA MORITZ

In the *Sermons on the Song of Songs*, Bernard of Clairvaux identifies the Bride, whose marriage the Song celebrates, as a figure both for the Church and for the individual soul. Bernard's 'spiritual' application of the text to the union of Christ and the Church usually remains of secondary importance to modern scholars,[1] because they regard the Sermons as a program for the soul's achievement of private, contemplative union with God. Bernard's application of the Song to the soul is undoubtedly central to the Sermons and represents one of Bernard's principal contributions to the history of Song of Songs literature. Still, the real significance of Bernard's instructions to the soul is lost if they are separated from what Bernard says about the mystical union of Christ and the Church. When he first identifies the subject of the Song, Bernard places the marriage of Christ and the Church before the union of Christ and the soul. Furthermore, when Bernard interprets a text under two explicitly different allegorical senses, he consistently speaks first of the Church and Christ and then uses their union as a model for the relationship which he urges the individual soul to seek. Throughout the Sermons, generally, Bernard bases his commentary on the conviction that Christ's union with the Church, accomplished by his coming in time, channels the grace of salvation to men in all times, and that the personal interaction of Christ and his Church provides a temporal witness and example of love God wishes to share with every soul. When Bernard's spirituality is evaluated in the context of his teaching on the Church as Bride, it is revealed to be free of the contradictions and tensions between contemplation and action, between withdrawal from and participation in this world, which many observers claim to have discovered in his life and teachings.

This paper will examine Bernard's Sermon Nine for its exposition of the phrase from the Song, 'your breasts are better than wine,' because this sermon's praise of the Bride marks a significant departure from commentary tradition, which in turn witnesses to the unprecedented dignity and responsibility Bernard attributes to the Bride as lover. Bernard's exposition, here as elsewhere, depends on his conviction that the Church is Christ's true bride, in the fullness of union; from the example of the Church, Bernard draws the lesson that love of Christ imparts not only personal completion but also the power and duty to undertake, with Christ, loving care for all men.

Bernard interprets the phrase 'your breasts are better than
wine,' as a speech which the Bride could have addressed to the Bridegroom, but which also might have been said to her by the Bridegroom
or his companions. He explains: 'We are free to assign these words
to the person whom we think they best suit. For my part, I can see
reasons for attributing them either to the Bride or to the Bridegroom or to the latter's companions.'[2] Although the text gave Bernard no guidance on the correct attribution of this remark, the commentary tradition of the Song furnished him with a consensus that
the Bride was speaking to the Bridegroom. Bernard reflects this tradition when he praises the Bridegroom's breasts as 'two proofs of
his native kindness: his patience in awaiting the sinner and his
welcoming mercy for the penitent.'[3] Bernard may also have borrowed
some materials from the previous comments on this phrase to formu-
late his praise of the Bride's breasts, but he makes a marked departure from his authorities in that he specifically states that the
Bride is here being honored.[4]

The quality of the Bride which Bernard finds celebrated in the
phrase 'your breasts better than wine,' is not a beauty or an ability to satisfy her lover, intrinsic to herself, as it was in the
case of the Bridegroom. Rather, both the Bridegroom and his companions praise the breasts of the Bride because in them they per-
ceive a proof that the Bride has achieved a full love-union with her
Beloved and been transformed by this exchange of love. The result
is that the Bride, filled by love, overflows with affection and understanding which may benefit others not yet proficient in loving
Christ. Bernard says, 'Our breast expands as it were, and our interior is filled with an overflowing love; and if somebody should
press upon it then, this milk of sweet fecundity would gush forth
in streaming richness.'[5] The Bridegroom's companions address the
Bride to urge her to recognize that this infusion is a favor given
for the sake of others: 'The favor you demand is rather for your
own delight, but the breasts with which you may feed the offspring
of your womb are preferable to, that is, they are more essential
than, the wine of contemplation.'[6] Here, Bernard not only departs
from tradition by explicitly praising the Bride, but he also gives
surprising priority to the Bride's loving service to others. He
places this loving care after, not prior to, a full sharing of
Christ's kiss, and he treats it as a progression toward union with
Christ, rather than a falling away from union.

Modern commentators tend to respond to spiritual texts which
use physical imagery by leaving the text and its literary tradition
in order to search for the attitudes, or the delusions, of the author about women, marriage, or the world, so that they can use
these attitudes to explain the author's selection and development
of allegorical images.[7] There are two shortcomings to this method:

first, a text's own unity of theme and image is not consulted for
what information it may give on any particular image, with the result that interpretations of particular images contradict the synthesis of theme and language for which the image was originally
created; second, wholly plausible, even explicitly stated, reasons
a medieval author might have had for his allegorizations are forgotten or ignored, while scholars seek what he 'really intended'
or 'unconsciously betrayed' in his imagery.

There has been some interest in the text under consideration
here because of Bernard's attribution of feminine characteristics
to Christ; the imagery is examined in the expectation that it will
reveal Bernard's views on women and marriage, which are presumed to
be the source for any images of women or feminine characteristics
he uses.[8] At least in Sermon Nine, literary tradition, rather than
personal observation or insight, lies behind what Bernard says about
the breasts of the Bridegroom. Commentators from Origen onward had
applied the words of praise to the Bridegroom; the frequency with
which they allude to other biblical texts in which the breasts of
God are praised suggests that the rationale behind the interpretation was that Scripture consistently used this figure to represent
divine mercy and compassion.[9] Furthermore, commentators consistently chose so to assign the speeches in the Song that praise and
thanksgiving were addressed to the Bridegroom, God, as the source
of all love, while expressions of longing, lack, or desire were
spoken of the Bride, either by the Bride herself or by the Bridegroom.[10]

Bernard's unconventional application of the phrase to the Bride
has excited less comment, perhaps because scholars have supposed
that it would be as natural and as logical for Bernard as it is for
them to direct praise of a feminine attribute to the Bride, a feminine figure. The fact that medieval exegetes shied away from making
this connection should alert us to the significance and originality
of Bernard's interpretation. Although certain elements from what
previous commentators said in praising the breasts of the Bridegroom
are echoed in Bernard's praise of the Bride, still Bernard transforms these materials by applying them explicitly to the soul, as
Bride. Gregory the Great, for example, had identified the breasts
of the Bridegroom as holy preachers; Bernard says that the breasts
of the Bride 'flow in the preaching of God's word.'[11] The importance of the shift is that Bernard directs attention to the role
the Bride plays, in union with Christ, as a source for the diffusion of God's love and knowledge in the world.

Sermon Nine employs an extended metaphor of pregnancy and
child-care in order to represent, first, the witness the Bride
carries in herself that she has shared the fullness of Christ's
kiss, and, second, the capacity she possesses, because of her love,

to share Christ with others. We have already seen that Bernard is
not here speaking only from the traditional practice of commenting
on the Song. Further, Bernard goes beyond the literal situation of
the Song, which follows the lovers only as far as the consummation
of their marriage, to present images of the bride's fecundity and
nurturing of children.[12] Any effort to attribute this imagery to
Bernard's own family life or his appreciation of human marriage,
as he had observed it around him, however, clashes immediately
with Bernard's explicit contrasts between physical, worldly experiences of love and nurturing, and the spiritual realities he is discussing. 'Here is a further reason why I insist that the breasts
of the bride are superior to worldly or carnal love; the numbers
who drink of them, however great, cannot exhaust their content;
their flow is never suspended.'[13]

The key to the image is the idea the image was fashioned to
represent. Bernard is describing a love which embraces the fullness of union between partners and which inspires them to bring
their united love into all their activities. This is the ideal of
love which he holds before the soul as a goal never to be realized
fully in this life, but it is an ideal which he observes as a temporal reality in the Church as the Bride of Christ. In his alle-
gorization of the breasts of the Bride, Bernard most resembles Origen, who mentions, without elaboration, that Christ could have directed this praise to his Bride, the Church, although not to individual, sinful souls.[14] Bernard follows Origen in basing his description of the love celebrated in the Song on the Church's relationship with Christ; as a result, Bernard speaks on a love union
already realized in marriage, already consummated and already fruit-
ful in offspring. The soul, although it may never achieve in this
world the fullness of love, still is directed to work toward that
achievement, in the Church.[15]

Bernard makes the analogy between the Church's love union with
God, and the soul's spiritual marriage, explicit in Sermons Sixty-
seven to Sixty-nine, which interpret the Bride's speech, 'My Beloved to me, and I to him.' Bernard argues that the Church may speak
so boldly of a reciprocity in love, because 'the Lord has need of
her.'[16] Although the Church may not claim a priority in love and
must admit that, at every moment, the Lord anticipated the Church
and prepared her to love, still Bernard finds that the Church by
loving God, satisfies God's need as well. The need the Church can
satisfy is to bring to God the communion of saints, restored from
death of sins, to complete heaven. Bernard says, 'Heaven has no
children. They belong only to the Church, to whose children it was
said, "I gave you milk to drink, not meat." And it is these who
are invited by the Prophet to complete the praises of God, where he
says, "Praise the Lord, ye children."'[17] Bernard describes the love

relationship of soul and Christ which entitles the soul to speak also
the words, 'My Beloved to me, and I to him,' in terms analogous to
those he has used of the Church. In common with the Church, the individual soul can claim no love of God that anticipated or preceded
God's love, yet the soul can return this love and also serve God's
need by caring for all men. The analogy is noteworthy, not only because Bernard establishes a parallel between Church and soul, but also because he identifies them as one and the same, that is, the
Church is the community of believers,[18] and all believers must share
in the work of the Church.[19]

Even in those passages in which Bernard does not speak explicitly of the Church as the Bride, his understanding of the Church's love
union with Christ as the exemplary model for all men's love for God
is central. Bernard's evident optimism and confident call to all
men to follow him in loving and serving God may have stemmed, personally, from experiences of contemplative union with God, but he does
not urge other men to optimism by his own example as a mystic or by
holding out the hope that all will be revealed through contemplation.
Rather, his trust in Christ's love begins with the historical fact
of Christ's coming and depends on Christ's establishment of the Church,
to whom he sent his Spirit as an abiding presence. The opening sermons on the Song especially ground Bernard's belief that the Bride en-
joys the fullness of Christ's love in the events of salvation history,
which joined Christ to his Bride, the Church, in a relationship which,
Bernard says, has never since ceased to be filled with love.[20] The
role of the Church, as mystical Bride, is both to witness to the proper conduct of a lover and also to channel to men the grace which en-
ables them to love.

The strategy of teaching which Bernard employs throughout the
Sermons is based on his conviction that God has chosen to bring men
to himself by manifesting himself to them in time, through a joining
of the Spirit and the flesh. This union was accomplished perfectly
in the Incarnate Christ alone.[21] Still, the fullness any creature
might possess of this love is known and shared, in time, by the
Church, as the Bride of Christ. Bernard consistently directs his
readers to the understanding and love of God accessible to them in
the Church. The allegorical language he employs is grounded in the
Church's Scriptures and in the Word made flesh. If we look for what
Bernard has learned about God's love from his observations of material, visible love relationships, we will be disappointed by the
shortcomings of the flesh which a comparison between it and the
spirit makes explicit. Bernard's language, however, has a different starting point: he seeks to make all things new in the spirit,
and so fashions a language which challenges creation to realize in
every activity the love God gives. What Bernard teaches about love
as a reciprocal sharing and a principle of conduct which may guide

lovers in all their activities is applied by Bernard directly only
to the particular life-style of the celibate monk, but, properly
understood, it is a view of loving which could be applied profit-
ably to the love men and women share in marriage.

In *The Great Chain of Being*, Arthur O. Lovejoy contrasts two
theories of value which might have been drawn from the medieval
philosophies of God as the source of all love.

> The one program demanded a withdrawal from all attach-
> ment to creatures and culminated in the ecstatic con-
> templation of the indivisible Divine Essence; the other,
> if it had been formulated, would have summoned men to
> participate, in some finite measure, in the creative
> passion of God, to collaborate in the processes by
> which the diversity of things, the fullness of the uni-
> verse, is achieved.[22]

He goes on to say that the Middle Ages chose the first program,
making ascent to the Good and escape from the many to the one the
ideal of all human activity. Lovejoy is speaking of sharing in
God's joy in creation, not only the act of creating but also the
existence of creation in all its diversity. Although Bernard of
Clairvaux would be considered by many scholars to be perhaps the
most influential medieval spokesman for love as contemplation, he
is, in fact, an innovative and challenging spokesman for a program
very much like Lovejoy's alternative love as sharing in God's creativity. It is not so much creativity as redemption which Bernard
asks the soul to share with God, and Bernard expects the creature
to delight as much in being God's creature as in his role of sharing God's tasks of loving and caring for creation. Still, Lovejoy's categories are helpful, because they demonstrate that the
core of Bernard's teaching on love is not love as longing, as escape, as frustrated desire, but rather love as possession, as en-
joyment, as fecundity and shared responsibility.

The University of Toronto

NOTES

1. Corneille Halflants, 'Introduction,' to *On the Song of Songs I*, tr. Kilian Walsh, Cistercian Fathers Series: 4 (Cistercian Publications, 1976) p. x; Jean Leclercq, *The Love of Learning and the Desire for God*, tr. K. Misrahi (New York: Fordham U. P., 1960) pp. 107-109. These are offered as formulations of a widely-held view.

2. SC 9; SBOp 1:44; PL 183:816 (CF 4:55-6): 'Et haec verba cujus sint, auctor non loquitur, relinquens nobis libere commentari, cui potissimum personae conveniant. Mihi vero non deest, unde illa congruenter assignem sive sponsae, sive sponso, sive etiam sponsi sodalibus.'

3. SC 9; SBOp 1:45; PL 183:817 (CF 4:57): 'Duo sponsi ubera, duo in ipso sunt ingenitae mansuetudinis argumenta, quod et patienter exspectat delinquentem, et clementer recipit poenitentem.' Many commentators, including Origen, Gregory the Great, Ambrose, Bede, Rupert of Deutz and William of St Thierry, speak of the breasts of the Bridegroom. See below, for more specific parallels between Bernard and other commentators.

4. Although Origen suggests that the phrase might be applied in some limited sense to the Church as Bride, he does not elaborate the significance of such an attribution to the extent that Bernard does. Origen's dual sense of the text, referring both to Christ and to the Church, was not often repeated before Bernard. Marian interpretation, such as that offered by Rupert of Deutz, in his *Commentaria in Cantica, Liber* 1; *PL* 168: 841, or by Honorius of Autun, in his *Expositio in Cantica Canticorum*; *PL* 172: 361, may have also suggested to Bernard the possibility of applying the phrase both to Christ and to the Bride.

5. SC 8; SBOp 1:46; PL 183:818 (CF 4:58): 'Persistentibus autem repente infunditur gratia, pingescit pectus, replet viscera inundatio pietatis; et si sit qui premat, lac conceptae dulcedinis ubertim fundere non tardabunt.'

6. SC 9; SBOp 1:47; PL 183:818 (CF 4:59): 'Quod enim postulas, te quidem delectat; sed ubera, quibus parvulos alis, quos et paris, meliora, hoc est necessariora, sunt vino contemplationis.'

7. Leclercq, in *Love of Learning*, pp. 95-96, alludes to the dangers

of this approach, although his own recent interest in psychological analysis of Bernard's views on marriage seems fraught with
the very dangers he had warned against previously. See *Nouveau
visage de Bernard Clairvaux: Approches psycho-historiques* (Paris:
Cerf, 1976). The practice is evident in the many books of feminist history devoted to ideas of love, women, and marriage,
during the Middle Ages, in which Bernard is condemned for his
anti-feminist position.

8. Caroline Bynum, 'Feminine Names for God,' a paper presented to
   the Conference on Consciousness and Group Identification in
   High Medieval Religion, held 6-8 April 1978, Toronto, Ontario.

9. Origen, *Homélies sur le Cantique des Contiques*, SC 376, 2nd
   edition, ed. Olivier Rousseau (Paris: Cerf, 1966) pp. 76-80,
   mentions other biblical stories in which the breast, or chest,
   of the Lord is a resting place for men. See Rupert of Deutz,
   Commentaria, and William of St Thierry, *Exposé sur le Cantique
   des Cantiques*, ed. J. M. Déchanet (Paris: Cerf, 1962) para.
   37, p. 122; *PL* 180:488.

10. Although the image itself might suggest that the author intend-
    ed a praise of women in their role as mother, the context of
    the image reveals that the intent of most commentators was to
    attribute the best of all qualities and activities to God and
    to leave for mankind only need and desire. Far from praising
    women, the image may serve to denigrate women's activities in
    the world, along with all other worldly activities as infinite-
    ly inferior to the spiritual realities of divine love. See be-
    low, n. 14.

11. Gregory the Great, in William of St Thierry's *Excerpta in lib-
    ris S. Gregorii papae suae super Cantica canticorum,* (*PL* 180:443)
    'Ubera sunt praedicatores sancti.' In Sermon 9, Bernard says,
    'Quia meliora sunt ubera praedicationis,' SBOp 1:47; PL 183:818
    (CF 4:59).

12. William of St Thierry, by comparison, denies that the marriage
    described is followed by physical consummation. *Exposé*, para.
    7, pp. 78-80; PL 180:455.

13. SC 9; SBOp 1:48; PL 183:819 (CF 4:60): 'Merito proinde meliora
    carnis, saeculive amore asseruntur ubera sponsae, quae nullo un-
    quam lactentium numero arefiunt, sed semper abundant de visceri-
    bus charitatis, ut iterum fluant.'

14. Origen, *Homélies*, pp. 72, 78.

15. See especially Sermon 50, on 'affective' and 'effective'
     charity.

16. SC 68; SBOp 2:199; PL 183:1110 (CF 40:21): 'Non ignorat quod
     Dominus se opus habet.'

17. SC 68; SBOp 2:199; PL 183:1110 (CF 40:21-2): 'Coelum non habet
     infantes, habet Ecclesia, quibus et dicit: "Lac vobus potum
     dedi, non escam." Et hi ad laudem quasi complendam a Propheta
     invitantur, dicente: "Laudate, pueri, Dominum."'

18. *Ibid.*

19. This is the theme of the many sermons Bernard preaches on the
     duties and responsibilities of Church officials, e.g., Sermons
     47, 51, 77, and many others.

20. Sermon 78, *passim*.

21. Sermon 2.

22. Arthur O. Lovejoy, *The Great Chain of Being* (Cambridge, Mass.:
     Harvard U. P., 1936) pp. 83-84.

ETHICAL THEORY IN THE SERMONS ON THE SONG OF SONGS

WILLIAM O. PAULSELL

In the third sermon of the Canticle series Bernard of Clairvaux warned his monks not to expect immediate mystical experience.
Using the kiss image he said that between the kiss of the foot
(*osculum pedis*) which is repentance and the kiss of the mouth
(*osculum oris*) which is mystical union there is the kiss of the
hand (*osculum manus*) by which Christ raises people to newness of
life. There is, he insisted, a relationship between the way one
lives and the mystical vision. Consequently, these sermons on
the mystical life have a strong ethical content.

The abbot of Clairvaux was clearly aware of the human condition, that sinfulness was an ever present reality.

> We all bear. . .the brand of that ancient conspiracy;
> Eve still lives in our flesh, and the serpent strives
> without ceasing, through the concupiscence which we
> derive from birth, to make us consenting parties to
> his rebellion.[1]

But man is made in the image of God, and one implication of
the *imago Dei* is freedom of the will (*arbitrii libertas*). Man
alone, among all living things, is free. This freedom of the will,
Bernard said, is

> a quality plainly divine, which shines forth in the
> soul like a jewel set in gold. It is by this that
> there is in the soul the power of distinguishing
> and the freedom of choosing between good and evil,
> that is, between life and death, between light and
> darkness, and other things similarly opposed, which
> present themselves to the consciousness of the soul.[2]

Man is, however, a fallen creature. The fall and the inabil-
ity to rise again are the fault of the will. If the will is in
servitude to sin, it is a willing servitude. 'If then,' said Bernard, 'it has made itself a slave voluntarily, it is also voluntarily that it remains in bondage.'[3]

The image of God has not been destroyed in man, but another
likeness has been laid over it.

> The soul has plainly not put off its original form,
> but has put on over it one which is foreign to it.

The latter is added, but the former is not lost. . .
The pure and simple nature of the soul remains unshaken
in its essential character, but it is concealed from
view by a thick film of human fraudfulness, and pretense, and hypocrisy.[4]

Voluntary servitude does not destroy the freedom of the will, then,
and man is capable of merit.[5] Ethical living is possible for man,
particularly under the power of grace.

In the Canticle sermons there seem to be seven major compo-
nents in the making of an ethical decision.

I.

First, an ethical decision must be made on the basis of charity and love of one's neighbor. Charity, said Bernard, is the
whole subject of the Canticle.

Love speaks in it everywhere, and if anyone desires to
obtain a knowledge of those things which are read in it,
a spirit of love is necessary to him that he may do so.
In vain will one who is without love attempt to listen
or read this Song of Love; the cold heart cannot com-
prehend or appreciate its language, full of feeling and
fire.[6]

The basis of all Christian ethics is the admonition to love
one's neighbor. This love has its beginning, said Bernard, 'in
the deepest feeling of human nature; and from the deeply-seated
principle of love to oneself.' With the gift of grace this love
develops into love for others, 'so that what the soul naturally
desires for itself, it considers not to be denied to another.'[7]

Bernard found the love of self to be the reason for the love
of neighbor. The neighbor, he said 'is that which you are; he is
man, as you are.' And if a person loves himself only because he
loves God, it would follow that he would love all those who also
love God.[8]

In Sermon twelve Bernard described the third perfume of the
Bride, *pietas*. This perfume was distilled from the individual's
compassion for

the necessities of the poor, the cares of the oppressed,
the disquiets of the sorrowful, the faults of the sinners, and finally from the misfortunes of those who are
unhappy.[9]

The happy soul, Bernard told his monks, was the one who was

> so imbued with the dew of mercy, so endued with chari-
> table affections, so rendering [itself] all things to
> all men, so regarding [itself] as but a broken vessel,
> that [it may] be at the service of others, and assist
> them in their need, whensoever and wheresoever it may
> be; and who, finally, [is] dead to [itself], that [it
> may] live to the benefit of all.[10]

And in Sermon sixty he praised the person

> who acts in union and peace with others, who lives
> among his brethren, not only without giving ground
> of complaint to any, but approving himself kind and
> helpful to all and fulfilling towards them every
> office of charity.[11]

Citing Matthew **twenty-five**, Bernard said that the person who
sins against his neighbor also sins against Christ. And, it is
not enough to avoid serious offences, one must also **abstain** from
secret whispers (*a clandestino et venenato susurrio*) against others.

> . . .even slight injuries to others ought to be avoided
> if indeed we can call any fault slight, which is done
> with the intent of injuring a brother, since according
> to the word of our Saviour, if anyone is angry with his
> brother without cause, for this alone he shall be in
> danger of the judgment.[12]

Bernard instructed his monks not to retaliate when they received an injury. They should not make any hostile response or
use 'cutting or ironical words' nor

> make surly answer nor grumble under your breath, nor
> take a sneering air, nor laugh mockingly, nor knit
> your brows, as if in wrath or threatening. Let your
> anger die away where it is born--do not permit it
> even to show itself, for it brings death with it.[13]

Elsewhere he said that his monks would be fragrant with the
richest perfume if they would be patient with the weaknesses of
their brothers and, beyond that, assist them to overcome their in-
firmities of body or mind.

Like a sweet balm in the mouth, is such a brother as
this in a community; he is pointed out with the finger
as a wonder, and all say of him: This is a lover of
the brethren, who prays much for the people.[14]

The most difficult element in brotherly love is, of course, love
of one's enemy. Bernard knew this and tried to encourage his men.

It is no small proof of virtue to live a good life a-
mong the depraved, to preserve the pureness of inno-
cence and gentleness of character among the evil-
disposed; it is still greater to be peaceful with
those who are hostile to peace, and to show yourself
a friend to your enemies themselves.[15]

Even if the enemy does not love God, one can love him in the
hope that he will learn to love God. One must think of the enemy,
not as he is now, but as he someday might be. Although it might
be clear that the individual will never love God, Bernard reminded
the brothers that 'charity, which is jealous in this respect, does
not allow that you should refuse to any man, even your most bitter
enemy, some small measure of affection' (*quantulumcumque affect-
um*).[16]

Bernard stressed the importance of charity in action (*caritas
in actu*) as opposed to charity of feeling (*caritas in affectu*) only. Commandments to love enemies, to feed them, and to do good
works to those who hate us are directives relating to actions, not
affections.[17] We ought not to be without feelings of charity, but
our feelings should be consistent with Divine Law and seasoned by
wisdom.[18]

For example, Bernard insisted that charity not be unbridled,
but that it be regulated by discretion (*discretio*).

The more fervent the zeal, the more eager the temper,
the more profuse the charity; the more need there is
of a watchful knowledge, which moderates zeal, tempers
the warmth of the disposition, and regulates the gush-
ings of charity.[19]

Bernard used his own duties as an example. His first obligations were to his own community, but he realized that other responsibilities beyond the monastery might, at times, be more important.
Discretion, the order of charity, might, on occasion, require that
matters in the world have the first claim on his time.[20] 'True
charity consists in this,' he wrote, 'that those whose needs are
greatest receive first.'[21]

In the context of discretion Bernard spoke of those who ruled
over others and praised those who sought no gain in the situation.
The ideal ruler was one who 'has drunk the wine of charity to the
point of condemning his own glory, and of entire forgetfulness of
himself, so that he seeks not his own.'[22]

In a later sermon he praised one responsible for others who
'seeks not the advancement of his own interests, or that which is
of advantage to himself, but that which is useful and beneficial
to many.' The reason Peter was given the care of the church, Bernard said, was that he cared so little for his own soul that he
was ready to go to prison or death if necessary. Paul was given
missionary responsibilities to the nations because he was ready
to die at Jerusalem for the name of Christ.[23]

The commandment to love, Bernard knew, was impossible to ful-
fil perfectly in this life. It exceeded man's ability. But it
was given to call attention to human weakness and to make man humble. So, man's salvation shall come not by works of righteousness
but by the mercy of God.[24]

                              II.

Second, Bernard advocated devotion to Christ as a factor in
making ethical decisions. In Sermon forty-three he said, 'In a
word, my philosophy is this, and it is the loftiest in the world,
to know Jesus and him crucified.'[25]

Christ's example was the model for Christian ethics. In Sermon twenty-one Bernard encouraged the brothers to follow the foot-
steps of Christ's life, to emulate his virtues, to hold fast to
his rule of life, and to attain His perfection of character.[26] In
Sermon sixteen Bernard lifted up Christ as 'an example of good
works.' and said, 'he has set my hands to great and noble deeds,
that he might teach my hands to war and my fingers to fight.'[27]

The name of Jesus was invoked as a way to restrain anger, re-
press pride, cure envy, bridle the impulse of luxury, and destroy
the desires of the flesh. Bernard said

When I utter the Name of Jesus, I set before my mind
. . .a man meek and humble in heart, moderate, pure,
benign, merciful, and, in short, conspicuous for every
honourable and saintly quality.

From him, inasmuch as he is man, I derive an example;
inasmuch as he is the Mighty One, I obtain assistance.
Of his example I make, as it were, medicinal and sal-
utary herbs, and his help is an instrument to prepare

them; thus I obtain a remedy of power, such as none
among physicians is able to compound.[28]

In Sermon twenty-two Bernard stressed the forgiving character
of Christ:

> We follow after [you], O Lord Jesus, because of the
> goodness and kindness which we are fully assured of
> finding in [you], because we learn that [you do] not
> despise the poor, nor abhor the sinner. [You] did
> not abhor the thief when he confessed, the sinful
> woman who wept tears of penitence, the Canaanite
> mother who came to [you] with her supplication, nor
> her who was taken in adultery, nor him who sat at
> the receipt of custom, nor the publican who implored
> pardon, nor the disciple who denied [you], the per-
> secutor of [your] disciples, nor the very crucifiers
> themselves. In the fragrance of these divine vir-
> tues we run.[29]

III.

Third, Bernard stressed the importance of purity of heart in
making ethical decisions.

In Sermon thirteen he pointed out that men 'of the most abandoned class' (*homines sceleratissimi*) give thanks to God for the
crimes they commit. The successful thief says, 'Thank God, I have
not made fruitless watches, nor spent my night to no profit!' The
murderer offers thanks that 'he has prevailed against his adversary,
or avenged himself of his enemy.' Even the adulterer 'thanks God
that he has obtained his long hoped for pleasure.' But, Bernard
warned, the only thanksgiving that is acceptable to God is that
which comes from a pure and sincere heart.[30]

He complained of hypocrites who glorified God with their lips,
but in their hearts praised themselves. They attributed to God
their bad actions and to themselves the good they might have done.
It is, Bernard said,

> a great and rare virtue to have no consciousness of
> greatness, although performing great actions; and that
> the sanctity of a man, while it is manifest to all
> others, should be hidden from himself. To appear ad-
> mirable to others, and to think humbly of yourself,
> this I judge to be the most marvellous among virtues
> themselves.[31]

Bernard urged his monks to 'go forward with free steps of a mind purified from evil passions.'[32]

In Sermon twenty-four Bernard warned that 'unrighteousness is a vice of the heart, not of the flesh.'[33] Faith and actions revealed the real condition of the mind.

> Consider him to be upright whom you have ascertained
> to be catholic in faith and righteous in actions. If
> one of these two be wanting, do not hesitate to con-
> clude that he is deficient in uprightness.[34]

Faith and works cannot be divided from each other. While faith without works is dead, Bernard also said, 'Neither do works, however upright they be, suffice, without faith, to render the heart upright.'[35]

In Sermon twenty-seven Bernard reiterated the connection between ethics and the knowledge of God. If one would contemplate God in peace or see Him as He is, one 'must be free from all hatred, all jealousy, all bitterness, for into a malicious soul wisdom shall not enter.'[36]

IV.

A fourth factor in Bernard's ethical theory is probably the best known, the element of right intention (*sana intentio*). In Sermon seven Bernard warned that virtue has no merit before God without a pure intention which is a desire to please God only.[37] Later, in Sermon seventy-one, he said

> The intention of the heart and the judgment of the con-
> science of the doer give an action its color.[38] If
> there be any spot upon the intention, it will not fail
> to appear also upon that which the intention has pro-
> duced; for the fault of the root appears in the bran-
> ches.[39]

Intention has two elements: The first is the act of the will, the thing intended; the second is the reason for the act, why it is intended. These two elements reflect the 'excellence or the defect of the soul.' If either element is lacking there is in the soul a 'want of symmetry which that defect causes.'[40] In fact, Bernard believed that without rightfulness of intention one is defrauded of life and salvation.[41]

'To have some degree of regard for God, yet not to act wholly for the sake of God' is the mark of an insincere soul. To direct

the mind to something other than God is the trouble of Martha, not
the response of Mary. Such a soul may not necessarily be deformed,
but it has not reached 'the perfection of beauty.'[42]

It is possible, of course, for some people to do good without
actually intending it. This brings no merit to the individual, but,
'God sometimes does good to the just by means of evil men.'[43]

There are occasions where a person faces opposition that comes
from a friendly intention. 'How many do we know of daily.' Bernard
wrote, 'who are led on to a higher standard and to a far stricter
mode of living by the pious rebukes of their superiors?'[44] Sometimes we benefit when evil is done to us. Opposition to the Church
has often made it stronger, even if the intention was evil.

Preaching, for example, can be done unethically if the intention is not pure. Bernard cited the man

> who makes a traffic of the Gospel, . . .who preaches
> the Gospel as a means of livelihood; to whom gain is
> godliness; and who does not seek for spiritual fruit
> provided he obtains a gift. Such as these are want-
> ing in pure intention; and though their mixture of
> motive hinders their beholding the truth, it does
> not hinder their discoursing of it as if they did be-
> hold it.[45]

Good intention also determines the quality of the monastic
life. Fasting for self-will (*voluntas propria*) rather than in
obedience will not be accepted by the bridegroom. The same is
true of silence, vigils, prayer, reading, manual labor, and all
monastic observances. If done, not in obedience, but from self-
will, they cease being good. Bernard said, 'Self-will is a great
evil, since it causes your good works not to be good for you.
Such works need to become lilies, for he who feeds among the lilies will not taste anything defiled by self-will.'[46]

V.

A fifth element in ethical conduct is discipline. It would
be better, of course, if one could live in peace with his brothers
simply because one had a 'spontaneous disposition to do so.' But
this is not always a realistic possibility. Discipline is necessary because if left to their own devices many people would 'not
be able to remain even peaceful and harmless to their neighbors.'[47]

In Sermon twenty-three Bernard discussed the three storerooms
of the king. The second and third were nature and grace, but the
first was discipline, an important element in the development of

ethical living. In discipline, he said, 'you learn, following the
rule of Christian ethics, to be last of all.' Having been corrupt-
ed by pride, most people wanted to be superior to others and thus
provoked one another. So, Bernard taught his monks that

> insolence of character (*insolentia morum*) requires to
> be restrained by the yoke of discipline, until the
> stubborn will, worn down by observance of the severe
> and constantly repeated rules of the elders, may be
> humbled and cured, and regain by its obedience that
> good of nature which it has lost by the indulgence of
> pride, until the man shall have learned to possess
> his soul in patience, and to live peacefully and kind-
> ly, so far as in him lies, with his fellow creatures.[48]

Bernard saw discipline as a way to punish the evil within.
'I will take care to correct the evil by better actions, to wash
it away by tears, to punish it be fasts and other actions of holy
discipline.'[49]

VI.

Sixth, we would expect a monk to insist on humility as an in-
gredient in ethical conduct. The Christian must be subject 'to
every human creature for the sake of God.' The monk, of course,
must be subject to his superiors, but that was not enough for Bernard. One must be subject to his equals and even to his inferiors.
'If then,' Bernard said, 'you wish to be perfect in righteousness,
make the first step towards him who is less than you; defer to
your inferior, show respect towards your juniors.'[50]
Great graces, Bernard insisted, cannot be obtained without the
merit of humility. When one is humbled, it is a sign that grace is
being given.[51]

VII.

Finally, Bernard believed that no good act could be performed
without the grace of God. It is grace that makes abstinence from
sin a possibility in the future. The kiss of the hand represents
a

> gift of grace, whereby I abstain from sin for the
> future, so that I may not again commit crime upon
> crime, and my last state be worse than the first.

Woe to me if he, without whom I can do nothing, shall
suddenly withdraw his supporting hand from me, even in
the midst of my penitence! Nothing, I repeat, am I
capable of doing without him; neither to repent of the
past, nor to keep myself from fresh sin.[52]

Near the end of the Canticle series, in the next to last sermon, Bernard told his brothers that the ascent to the hill of the
Lord, which is the perfection of virtue, is an arduous one. It is
easy to fall without the help of the Word. The soul must not pre-
sume upon its own powers, but must be strengthened by Christ in order that it may rule over its own powers and not be dominated by unrighteousness.[53]

VIII.

What, then, are the rewards of ethical living? For one thing,
a virtuous life produces a better frame of mind. Depression, Bernard said, is often caused by 'lukewarmness of conduct.'[54]

Second, Bernard listed immortality as a reward. There is no
place 'in the soul for the life of immortal blessedness except that
which is provided by the means and the interposition of virtues.'[55]

A third reward of ethical living is the presence of Christ in
the soul. Likening virtuous actions to lilies, Bernard said, 'Take
heed that you have in your soul, and in your life, lilies that grow
and flourish, if you wish to have him who dwells among the lilies
dwelling in you.'[56]

Finally, the greatest reward is the contemplation of God.
Bernard told his monks,

Perhaps you desire also the repose of contemplation;
and in this you do well, provided that you do not
forget the flowers with which. . .the couch of the
Bride is strewn. Therefore. . .take great care
similarly to wreathe around [yourself] the blossoms
of good works, and to make the exercise of virtues
precede that sacred rest.[57]

The fruitfulness of Leah, he said, should not be neglected
just to enjoy the society of Rachel. That would be reversing the
proper order of things, for 'the taste of contemplation is not due
except to obedience to God's commandments.'[58]

Atlantic Christian College
Wilson, North Carolina

NOTES

1. Sermons on the Canticle, 72:8. The translation used is Samuel J. Eales, *Cantica canticorum: Eighty-six Sermons on the Song of Solomon by St Bernard*. (London: Elliot Stock, 1895). The critical Latin text is J. Leclercq et. al., *Sancti Bernardi Opera*, Vols. 1 and 2 (Rome: Editiones Cistercienses, 1957).

2. SC 81:6
3. 81:8
4. 82:2
5. 81:6
6. 79:1
7. 44:4
8. 50:7
9. 12:1
10. 12:1
11. 60:9
12. 29:4
13. 29:5
14. 12:5
15. 48:2
16. 50:7
17. 50:3
18. 50:4
19. 49:5
20. 49:6
21. 50:6
22. 23:8
23. 30:8
24. 50:2
25. 43:4
26. 21:2
27. 16:2
28. 15:6
29. 22:8
30. 13:2
31. 13:3

32. 13:7
33. 24:5
34. 24:7
35. 24:8
36. 27:10
37. 7:7
38. 71:7
39. 71:2
40. 40:2
41. 18:2
42. 40:3
43. 5:9
44. 30:1
45. 62:8
46. 71:14
47. 23:8
48. 23:6
49. 55:3
50. 42:9
51. 34:1
52. 3:3
53. 85:5
54. 10:9
55. 27:3
56. 71:1
57. 46:5
58. 46:5

HUMANISM IN BERNARD OF CLAIRVAUX:
BEYOND LITERARY CULTURE

EMERO STIEGMAN

Humanism, like all terms which historians invent to label a complex but broadly identifiable set of attitudes, is subject to ambiguity; the attitudes are affected by changing historical conditions. Since the common ground among humanisms develops in inverse proportion to the number which history records, one may come to question the usefulness of the label. Yet in religious thought humanism is a serviceable and perhaps necessary category. To Christian theologians, for example, an author would be humanistic to the extent that he validated the human. There are two foci of meaning --one, where the human is considered with respect to the divine (here humanism refers to a position on issues concerning the relation of nature and grace); the other, where the content and structure of the human itself is considered (here humanism refers to a position in anthropology, one which dignifies the body in a more unitary concept of body and soul, as against one which may be called spiritualistic, where all dignity is reserved for the soul in a more loosely conceived relationship of body and soul). The two foci sometimes move extremely close together.

Much contemporary Christian theology is humanistic by these meanings. It attempts to remedy, for example, what it thinks of as too extrinsicist a view of divine grace. And something of this humanism inspired an earlier generation of French commentators when they singled out Bernard of Clairvaux for the emotional warmth of his devotion to the humanity of Christ.

Something only. All told, they did not understand the full range of the theological context into which Bernard set this devotion, as the censures of J. Ch. Didier make clear.[1] The humanism attributed to Bernard was of merely superficial significance. With qualifications, something similar may be said of Edgar de Bruyne's concept of a Cistercian humanism:[2] It provides us with a considerably more appreciative understanding of Bernard's 'warmth', but does not take us beyond acknowledging the advantages of traditional monastic literary culture over a narrow intellectualism. What de Bruyne sees is there; Leclercq traces its continuity in the Benedictine tradition.[3] What could be further explored is whether a truly theological humanism in St Bernard underlies this cultural surface. The question is not idle. It is prompted by the grave difficulties regarding the spirituality of St Bernard to which some notable present-day readers have confessed. A more extensive awareness of Bernard's text, occasioned by several excellent academic celebrations of the eighth centenary of his death (1153),

has produced at times a one-hundred-eighty degree turn-about in
criticism of the abbot, from devotionalism to spiritualism. One
may be disturbed to hear Bernard exalt the soul so lyrically while
at the same time concluding that the kindest comment on the body is
to say nothing--*de corpore taceam* (11.5); or to hear him argue that
that by which man is like God, and that in which God takes delight,
is man's soul as distinguished from his body because, like the soul,
'God is spirit' (cf. Jn 4:24);[4] or that in contemplation, divine
wisdom is possessed, not in ideas or images, but in a wholly spiritual likeness, through *spirituales similitudines* (41.3). A comprehensive study of Bernard's uses of *homo* and *humanus* would demonstrate that these are virtually derogatory terms in his text.[5] He
does not exult in the human--only in the spiritual. Even a sympa-
thetic reader like Déchanet finds in this a 'dualism of flesh against
spirit.'[6] Congar speaks of an 'extremely spiritual conception of the
Christian life,'[7] and Chenu, with less sympathy, of a 'disincarnate
spiritualism.'[8] The spiritualist leaning may be seen as structuring
his thought to such an extent that the warmth of his literary personality loses all theological significance.

I would like to suggest, to the contrary, that the reason Bernard gratified his love for literature and then expressed human ideas
and emotions with serious artistry is that he possessed the central
attitude of the theological humanist--that is, a profound sense of
human worth. Christopher Brooke calls the student's attention, however vaguely, to a bernardine humanism beyond the literary. It con
stitutes, he confesses, 'the strangest paradox of all in St Bernard:
Austere as he was, he allowed free play to certain human emotions
...even, in the process, doing something to humanize the austerity
of medieval theology.'[9] Again: 'Bernard, if he had understood the
term, would have repudiated the label humanist. Yet...he seems to
have more in common with Abelard and Heloise than with many of his
contemporaries.'[10] Let us approach this 'strangest paradox' by
pointing out two areas of Bernard's thought where so strong a consciousness of a fully human self is valued and cultivated that an
effective counterpoise is set up in relation to elements which,
alone, might create an 'extremely spiritual conception of the Christian life.'[11] We shall consider first the process of Christian
growth; and, second, the genesis of human love--concentrating upon
the *Sermones super Cantica Canticorum*.

The Process of Christian Growth

Bernard's dynamic concept of the image of God in the soul is
an exalted view of the human self. He is repeatedly awed by this
relationship between the Word and the soul--'So close a kinship of
nature!' ('Naturarum tanta cognatio').[12] The Word is the truth,

wisdom, and justice of God, and the soul is 'capable and desirous of these' (*earundem capax, appetensque*).[13] The soul's *magnitudo* consists in this capacity for God; it can never be lost. But its *rectitudo*, the *appetere iustitiam*, is lost in sin. Most significant in man's possibility for self-respect is this notion that there is in the very construction of the soul a natural drive to God and a capacity for him. It is natural, in Bernard's view, because it is what God has made in the historical order.[14] By the activity of this 'appetite' for God, the *similitudo Dei*--the simplicity, immortality, and freedom which were partly lost in sin--is increased or restored[15] (see Sermons 80 through 82). The perfect soul is *similis ei.*

If we condense familiar stages of the process into a brief exposition, we shall be able to delineate St Bernard's conception of its normality.

The movement toward God in the soul begins in self-knowledge, in Christian Socratism.[16] The author writes: 'I want the soul to know itself first of all, because this is demanded both by reason of usefulness and by reason of order' (*Volo proinde animam primo omnium scire seipsam, quod id postulat ratio et utilitatis, et ordinis*).[17] The subject is studied under the text 'Si ignoras te, egredere' (Sg 1:8) from sermons 34 through 38.[18] Self-knowledge produces first an insight into the un-godly misery arising from false pride; this begets humility as the starting point of a love leading back to God.[19] If one stops at Bernard's description of the first data of self-knowledge,[20] one will not see the saint as optimistic; but this is a beginning. In the sermons the endless insistence upon realism in reflections upon asceticism is striking.[21] In the knowledge needed by the soul in search of God, there is little interest in an intellectual grasp of the nature of things in the abstract; usable knowledge, in this context, is not 'the truth,' but each man's truth. In the return to God Christ is the way, and advancement is measured by obedience. All asceticism is geared to a conformity of the will to God's will--'transformamur cum *conformamur.*'[22]

But characteristic of St Bernard is that at this point he does not insist upon the perseverance of the faithful drudge. It is not now simply a matter of effort: 'Neither diligence nor nature conquers malice; wisdom does' (*Sapientia vincit malitiam, non industria vel natura*).[23] And *sapientia* is the sweet taste of divine things, the experience beyond faith. Obviously, the meaning given to faith in such contrasts arises, not out of ontological reflection (where faith is true knowledge of God or personal engagement with him), but out of psychological experience (where it is suffered as inextricably bound up with human ignorance)--as one finds in St Paul's comparison of faith and hope to charity (1 Cor. 13:12-13). Bernard thinks of mere faith as a transition, and one

that will not be effective with 'human' beings very long. Life in
Christ must move beyond faith: 'Faith has been constructed; now
let life be brought forth' (*Aedificata est fides, instruatur vita*).[24]
Also the understanding necessary to move on from lowliness is an experiential *sapientia*. The companions of the bride, imperfect souls
--'quoniam minus *sapiunt*, minus et capiunt'--to the extent their
spiritual experience is thin, their perceptions dim.[25] Bernard, who
demands that men see things as they are, and is thus unflattering, be-
carries his realism to the point of seeing men as the affective beings they are, and in this is most compassionate, for he discovers
the realism of God's manner with men.

For example, he will say that to kiss the divine Bridegroom
the soul must ascend to the lips, kissing the feet and the hands
first. But the fear[26] and penance instilled at conversion, represented by the kiss of the feet,[27] are tempered by the abbot's advice that they not be continuous, lest the heart be overtaken by
sadness and be hardened again.[28] Then, fraternal charity is not
encouraged merely from a faith which is 'sicca sed fortis,'[29] but
from a consideration beginning in that natural human sympathy which
Bernard is confident will arise in self-knowledge--'Ex consideratione
suiipsius.'[30]

Asceticism as progress in the virtues is represented by the kiss
to the divine hands. The vices may be subjugated but not exterminat-
ed.[31] The renunciation of self-will is not a stage, but must continue through life, when fear has been replaced by love.[32] The union the soul seeks is a 'communio voluntatum.'[33] The vision toward
which the soul moves is charity: 'Caritas illa visio.'[34] The soul
meanwhile must be roused to effort, because the turning of the will
to God is the work of grace within the soul, but it is also the work
of the soul. The fruit of union comes only after the flower of virtue.[35] Effort, or psychic energy, is a great gift of nature, says
the abbot, and it must be employed: 'Ut quid enim dormitet *industria?*
Grande profecto in nobis *donum naturae* ipsa est.'[36] Even the ultimate kiss to the lips will be a *conformitas:* 'Conformity *marries*
the soul to the Word' (*talis conformitas maritat animam Verbo*)[37]
The ascetical progress and the final union are put in proper relationship with Bernard's oft-repeated, '*Similes ei* erimus, quoniam
videbimus eum sicuti est.'[38] Sermon 83 is a résumé of the entire
process.

This overview of Bernard's concept of Christian growth makes
possible certain considerations about the character of his asceticism. First, the structuring of the idea of the image of God in
the soul, according to which the soul has a capacity for and a
drive towards God, supplies a theology for the element of self-
reliance implicit in traditional monastic ascetical doctrine in the
West. Before, there may have been too pragmatic an acceptance of
the necessity of avoiding a *pax perniciosa*, a necessity which had

taken refuge in theories attacked as semi-pelagian.[39] In St Bernard,
the soul which does not strive frustrates a movement from within
which is indeed a movement of grace, but conceived as planted by
God in the very nature of the soul. A remarkably humanistic theological postulate! Second, the possibilities that Bernard sees in
self-knowledge indicate a strong sense of personhood. Even God is
known in the self, for there, more than in any of his other works,
his beauty is discovered and his call is heard. Third, the notion
that man grows toward God, according to a process which may be determined because it is the development of a dynamism that is within
him, is a notion of human grandeur. There are normal stages; the
fruit comes after the flower. This is an assumption in Bernardine
asceticism. The soul's industry is not the effective force in growth;
grace is. But grace will work through the soul's industry. This is
predictable on the grounds that the soul's effort in itself manifests
God's effective desire, preceding the soul's desire, to be united to
it. This emphasis on the normal is an emphasis upon a 'self' concept—a self who is addressed and who answers to the Word of God in
the dialogical drama of redemption as seen imaged forth in the dialogue of the Song of Songs.[40]

The Genesis of Human Love

One simple fact will account for the absence of any great preoccupation with an austerity problem in the thought of most commentators on St Bernard. These writers have seen the abbot's asceticism strictly in relation to his doctrine on love. We have several
excellent analyses of the Sermons, all of them centering upon Bernard's exposition of the ways of divine love—the most well-worked
theme in Bernardine scholarship.[41] Though it does not suit our purpose to allow the approach to dominate this enquiry, much of the
problem in the saint's ascetical language may, by appeal to doctrinal consistency, be bypassed in virtue of the clarity, force, and com-
prehensiveness of his teaching on love. Love stimulates the soul's
ascetical reflection and its effort, which is then undertaken in order to grow in this divine love. This understanding is indispensable.
But rather than attempting once again to document the fact that love
is the source, means, and the end of asceticism in the Sermons,[42]
let us look at yet another aspect of love. We can observe an important evidence of Bernard's strong and positive sense of the human
self in his concept of the genesis of human love (*amor carnalis*)
and of its function in the soul's divine aspirations.

Bernard conceives love as having four degrees of perfection;
the center shifting from self to God.[43] the imperfect beginning of
love is systematically described in *De diligendo Deo* and in *De
gratia et libero arbitrio*. 'Amor est *affectio naturalis*,' says

Bernard, 'una de quatuor.'[44] The *naturalis* is further explained:
'We possess naturally, from within ourselves, simple affective
motions; they become enriched by grace....Grace puts in order what
creation provided' (*Simplices namque affectiones insunt naturaliter
nobis, tamquam ex nobis, addimenta ex gratia....Gratia ordinat, quas
donavit creatio*).[45] This love is of man as *caro*, considered apart
from the salvific action of grace; it is, then, *amor carnalis*. With
this we justify the expression 'human love' as a clarification of
Bernard's *amor carnalis*. Bernard describes how far this love reaches:
'It is *amor carnalis* by which man loves himself before all things and
for his own sake' (*Est amor carnalis, quo ante omnia homo diligit
seipsum propter seipsum*).[46] This is the beginning of love, according
to a Bernardine law: 'Prius quod animale [that is, *ex anima*], deinde
quod spirituale.'[47] Here also is the logical antecedent of fraternal
charity, and in this sense its beginning: 'Sic amor *carnalis* efficitur et *socialis*, cum in commune protrahitur.'[48] As this human love
receives its *ordinatio* in grace, even as it progresses toward the
highest perfection of divine love, the self is not to be annihilated
or eliminated. The highest degree of love is that man should love
himself only for God: 'Nec seipsum diligat homo nisi propter Deum.'[49]
    Without an awareness of this highly developed Bernardine sense
of the fundamental role of natural affectivity, one cannot put into
proper perspective the 'spiritualism' according to which the soul,
participating in a 'kinship of natures' with God as spirit, is constituted with a natural appetite for him.[50]
    The love we have been describing does not bypass human resources;
it is clearly an *eros*--not an immediate leap to agape.[51] The love
treated of in the Sermons is what the author reads in the Song: 'Holy
love, which one observes to be the single subject of this entire book'
(*Amor sanctus*, quem totius huius voluminis unam constat esse materi-
am).[52] But in Bernard's advancing degrees of love, one does not destroy and replace the other; grace works through the *affectiones*. The
author feels compelled to make this explicit when he explains that
there are three kinds of love: 'This human love,' he says, 'is good
....It advances when it becomes rational as well; it is perfected when
it also becomes spiritual.'[53] We read extremely little in Bernard
about this 'rational' love, which the larger context reveals to be
proper of a faith not yet perfected in wisdom. The unfeeling condition of mere faith, he is persuaded, can be only a transition from the
affectivity of nature to the experience of the spiritual senses--that
is, of *sapientia*.[54] This stress on the role of human love (affirming,
as it does, what is of man) cannot be excluded from consideration when
one reacts to impressions of anti-humanist thought in some Bernardine
formulations. The emphasis is clearly perceived, though rejected, in
the Lutheran thought of Anders Nygren. 'The foundation of this view
of love,' Nygren says, 'is something as earthly and human, far too
human, as natural self-love.'[55] One who claims that Bernard slights

the human must ask whether Nygren's interpretation, though to the Roman Catholic mind it expresses an excess, does not force a re-examination of Bernard's spiritualism.

　　The two outstanding examples in the Sermons of this *eros* which becomes possessed by divine *agape* are Bernard's description of *amor carnalis socialis* as a channel of grace, and his discussion of *amor carnalis Christi*.　Notice in the first instance how the author, with perceptible feeling, dwells upon and develops the origin in nature of that which, 'spirante quidem gratia desuper' (under the breath of grace from above), becomes the Christian virtue *mansuetudo* (humble gentleness):

> In intimate human feelings fraternal love finds its primordial origin; and from that natural sweetness which is part of every man's disposition toward himself, as from moisture in the soil, it invariably receives the vigor by which it grows.　In this vigor, while grace breathes upon it from above, it brings forth fruits of gentleness, so that what one naturally desires for oneself, by a certain law of humanity, one would not consider denying to another man, a sharer of his nature; but when he was able and had the opportunity, spontaneously and freely would he share. There is then in nature, before sin dries it up, a free-flowing and excellent balsam of near-sweetness, softening man to feel himself one with other sinners rather than hardening him to feel that he is unlike them.[56]

　　This balsam is *quasi suavitatis* (of near-sweetness), for the author reserves *suavitas* for the experience of the Word in the soul.
　　Amor carnalis Christi, however, suffers no such qualification. Love for the *Verbum caro* gives rise to a true *suavitas*; it is already a grace:　'Although this kind of devotion to the humanity of Christ [*erga carnem Christi*] is a gift and a great gift of the Spirit,' says the author, 'I nevertheless call this love human [*carnalem*]--with respect to that love by which is experienced not only the Word as flesh but the Word as wisdom.'[57]　The very fact of the humanity of the Word[58] is spoken of as '*gratia* praesentis suae carnis.'[59]　Nevertheless, there is something of nature in love for Christ.　The author explains that the invisible God, knowing that men could not love *nisi carnaliter*, became a visible man among them in order to draw their love toward his humanity, 'atque ita *gradatim* ad amorem perduceret spiritualem.'[60]　As we have mentioned, Bernard's genial conception of the divine pedagogy of the Incarnation has not always been understood.[61]　It is precisely in the context of his most lyrical attempts to portray the humanity of Christ that

the abbot insists upon the necessary progression from *amor carnalis* to *amor rationalis* and *spiritualis*. He does not hesitate to apply to Christ 'Caro non prodest quidquam.'[62] Even in the satisfaction he takes in the imaginative projection of Christ's humanity, he does not relent in his drive toward a wholly spiritual contemplation. In attempting to understand so complex a literary personality, one must place beside this spiritual emphasis another clear fact of the text: In the cultivation of joy in the thought of the human Christ, the first classic is that Bernard who exclaims, 'How beautiful must I acknowledge you to be, Lord Jesus, as you assume my shape!' (Quam *formosum* et in *mea forma* te agnosco, Domine Iesu!).[63] And Bernard's concept of this satisfaction is that it is the spontaneous emotion of the natural man, *amor carnalis,* through which grace has chosen to operate.

It seems significant that, in the central matter of love for God and neighbor, Bernard gives importance, not only to that grandeur of a spiritual self which is the soul's capacity and desire for God, but to a special goodness of the psycho-physical self (*caro*) --that is, an affective energy which may be possessed by divine love. In the concept *amor carnalis*, he goes far beyond a grudging acknowledgment that man as *caro* is not evil because God created him. His theology of the genesis of human love is simply and profoundly humanistic.

Conclusion

I have offered what I believe to be the strictest criteria of a theological humanism. And I would contend, after this rapid exposition of two themes from the *Sermones super Cantica Canticorum*, that in these conceptions St Bernard is a humanist. In his view of the process of Christian growth, he validates the full range of human faculties as intrinsically instrumental to divine grace. In his view of human love, those affective motions which we today conceive of as operations of the psyche at the depth of its embodiedness --human feelings--initiate what becomes the love of God. This is the maximum validation of man's psycho-physical nature possible within Christian speculation.

Yet, when all is said, I shall not deny that St Bernard is in large part spiritualistic. Obviously, the way we conceptualize Christian experience is culturally conditioned. Every saint is fated to work within the philosophical assumptions of his age. But perhaps the more intimately an author's text grows out of authentic experience the more surely will it record elements of consciousness which are poorly integrated by the reigning philosophy. However offensive such a premise is to true believers in the Platonism of the Fathers, which suffuses Bernard's text, the premise allows or invites one to look for a larger Bernard than the one portrayed (falsely, I believe) by devotionalism on one side and (less falsely) by spiritualism on the other. It invites us to give weight to the two humanistic elements I have described here, and to recognize that, however inconsistently, crucial areas of Bernard's thought escape what might have been considered the hegemony of a spiritualistic system. We have seen that for Bernard certain primordial human feelings bespeak the operation of grace; in them God himself is at work loving those humans toward whom they instinctively move. This is rather unlike anything associated with the platonic *soma*. How splendidly inconsistent!

Inconsistency is, of course, an intellectual flaw. But in the great it is frequently the price paid for giving witness to all the data of experience. If St Bernard is, through a set of philosophical assumptions, a platonic spiritualist, he is, through the experiential depth of the saint and the unruly objectivity of the artist, a Christian humanist. As interpreters of each succeeding age ask themselves whether they have fitted his vision to their systems, their more difficult question may be whether they see all that he saw.

Saint Mary's University
Halifax, Nova Scotia

NOTES

1. See J.-Ch. Didier, 'La dévotion à l'humanité du Christ dans
la spiritualité de saint Bernard,' *La Vie Spirituelle, Supplé-
ment* (August-September, 1930) pp. [1] - [19]. This study of
St Bernard's devotion to the humanity of Christ suffers from
an unawareness that the saint proposes meditation on Christ's
humanity only as the natural starting point in the spirituali-
zation of love. What we say of love, below, should make that
clear. Didier chooses his central text well, sermon 20 of the
Sermones super Cantica Canticorum (SC), where Bernard speaks
most concretely and affectively of the human Christ.

     We too, in this paper, choose to work predominantly with
the SC. References to the work will be indicated in parentheses according to sermon and numbered paragraph—e.g. (20.7)
—using the edition of Jean Leclercq, C. H. Talbot, and H. M.
Rochais, Vols, I and II of *Santi Bernardi Opera*, eds. J. Leclercq and H. M. Rochais (Rome 1957-58).

2. See Edgar de Bruyne, *Etudes d'esthétique médiévale*, 3 vols.
(Bruges: Rijksuniversiteit te Gent, 1946), III: 38-57.

3. See Jean Leclercq, 'L'humanisme bénédictin du VIIIe au XIIe
siècle,' in *Analecta monastica* 1 (Rome, 1948) 1-20; R. W.
Southern has incorporated these views into his work, *The Mak-
ing of the Middle Ages* (London, 1953) pp. 203-207; as has R.
R. Bolgar in *The Classical Heritage and its Beneficiaries*
(Cambridge, England, 1954) pp. 117-18. Jean Leclercq expanded
his treatment of the literary humanism of the monks in *The
Love of Learning and the Desire for God: A Study of Monastic
Culture* (New York: Fordham, 1961) *passim*.

4. SC 4.4: 'Verum quia spiritus est Deus, et nullis simplex illa
substantia membris distincta corporis....' This understanding
of Bernard rests upon an examination of several texts in my un-
published dissertation, *The Language of Asceticism in St Bernard of Clairvaux's Sermones super Cantica Canticorum* (Ann Ar-
bor, Mich.: University Microfilms, 1973) pp. 131-35.

5. In *The Language of Asceticism* (n. 4, above) pp. 108-19, the
uses of *homo* and *humanus* are studied.

6. See J.-M. Déchanet, 'The Christology of Saint Bernard,' in
Saint Bernard Théologian, Cistercian Studies, I (May, 1961)
37 [an informal translation of 'La christologie de S. Bernard,'
Analecta Cisterciensia 9 (1953) 78-91].

7. Yves Congar, 'The Ecclesiology of Saint Bernard,' in *Saint Bernard Théologian, Cistercian Studies*, I (May, 1961), 89 ['L'ecclésiologie de S. Bernard,' *Analecta* 9 (1953) 136-190].

8. 'Le spiritualisme désincarné.' See M.-D. Chenu, *L'Evangile dans le temps*, Vol. 2 of *La Parole de Dieu*, 2 vols. (Paris, 1964) p. 562. See also 'The Platonisms of the Twelfth Century,' in *Nature, Man, and Society in the Twelfth Century*, translated by Jerome Taylor (Chicago, 1968) p. 62.

9. See Christopher Brooke, *Europe in the Central Middle Ages*, 962-1154 (London, 1975) p. 314. Problems in the meaning of humanism have been discussed by David Knowles, 'The Humanism of the Twelfth Century' (1941), and 'St Bernard of Clairvaux: 1090-1153' (1953), both in *The Historian and Character, and Other Essays* (Cambridge, 1963) pp. 16-30, 31-49; and by R. W. Southern, *Medieval Humanism, and Other Studies* (Oxford, 1970) pp. 29-132.

10. Brooke, p. 319.

11. Congar, p. 81.

12. SC 50.2. See P. Delfgauuw, 'La Lumière de la charité chez saint Bernard,' *Collectanea* 18 (1956) 42-69, 306-20. The author notes, regarding Bernard's astonishment at the grandeur of the soul, that *praesumere* is one of the saint's favorite words, occurring over one hundred times in his work.

13. SC 80.2. See 27.10.

14. See also SC 44.4, 82.5.

15. Sermons 80 through 82.

16. For a bibliography on Christian Socratism in Bernard, see Friedrich Ohly, *Hohelied-Studien* (Wiesbaden, 1958) p. 152, n. 2.

17. SC 36.5.

18. See *Dil.* II, 4, in SBOp 3:122.

19. J.-M. Déchanet, 'Les Fondements et les bases de la spiritualité Bernardine,' *Cîteaux in de Nederlanden* 4 (1953) 292-313. The author contrasts Bernard's more practical approach to self-knowledge with William of St Thierry's vision of a discovery of greatness.

20. SC 36.5.

21. H. von Balthasar, *Herrlichkeit* (Einsiedelm, 1961) I: 275, be-
    lieves Bernard saw in the oft-repeated statement 'Est enim
    sapiens cui quaecumque sapiunt prout sunt' (Div 19.1) the
    foundation of Christian spirituality.

22. SC 62.5. See Corneille Halflants, 'Le Cantique des cantiques
    de saint Bernard,' in *Collectanea* 15 (1953) p. 258.

23. SC 82.7. See Wis 7:30.

24. SC 17.8.

25. SC 19.7; see 8.6.

26. SC 6.8.

27. SC 3.2-3.

28. SC 11.2.

29. SC 50.4.

30. SC 44.4.

31. SC 37.1, 58.10.

32. SC 58.11. See Kurt Knotzinger, 'Hoheslied und bräutliche
    Christusliebe bei Bernhard von Clairvaux,' in *Jahrbuch für
    mystische Theologie* 7 (1961) 30.

33. SC 71.10.

34. SC 82.8.

35. SC 46.5.

36. SC 83.2.

37. SC 83.3.

38. SC 82.7; 1 fn 3:2.

39. Owen Chadwick, *John Cassian* (Cambridge, 1950) p. 186, says,
    regarding Augustine's attack against certain formulations of

Cassian: 'The first western ascetical theologian [Cassian] rejected Pelagianism....But neither he nor many of his medieval
successors clearly remàrked the reef which could wreck the
study of Christian asceticism, the translation into life itself of the *theoretical* abstraction from grace. The emphasis
is mine. See also Louis Bouyer et. al., *Histoire de la spiritualité chrétienne*, 4 vols. (Paris, 1960-66), where in I: 594-
95, Bouyer also remarks upon a lack of theological structure in
Cassian's practically oriented asceticism.

40. 'Ct. [Canticle] is dramatic in the sense that it is conceived as
dialogue.' Roland E. Murphy, 'Canticle of Canticles,' in Raymond
E. Brown, SS, Joseph A. Fitzmyer SJ, and Roland E. Murphy O.
Carm., ed., *The Jerome Biblical Commentary* (Englewood Cliffs,
N. J., 1968) I, art. 30:3. The 'drama' of personal redemption,
in which there is a type of conflict between a loving God and
obstinate man, does not seem to be typified in the Song by any
conflict or dramatic structuring beyond dialogue form.

41. J. Ries, *Das geistliche Leben in seinen Entwicklungstufen nach
der Lehre des hl. Bernhard*; J. Schuck, *Das Hohelied des hl. Bernhard von Clairvaux*; E. Gilson, *The Mystical Theology of Saint
Bernard*; J. Leclercq, *St. Bernard mystique*; Corneille Halflants,
'Le Cantique des cantiques de saint Bernard'; P. Delfgaauw, 'La
Lumière de la charité chez saint Bernard'; Kurt Knotzinger,
'Hoheslied und bräutliche Christusliebe bei Bernhard von Clairvaux.' Ohly, p. 149, n. 1, presents a bibliography on Bernard's
concept of love and on the history of the concept of *caritas
ordinata*.

42. Etienne Gilson, *The Mystical Theology of Saint Bernard*, translated by A. H. C. Downes (New York, 1940) p. 22.

43. Dil VIII-X; SBOp 3:138-44.

44. Dil, VIII, 23.

45. Gra VI, 17; SBOp 3:178. A good example of the pre-technical
character of Bernard's use of theological terminology may be
noticed in his use of *naturalis*. Here *naturalis* pertains to
what man receives in creation as distinguished from the elevation of redemptive grace. The image of God in the soul, however, is a 'natural' capacity for, and striving for, God (SC
80.2)--a concept of nature which is not distinguished from the
elevation of grace. It seems an over-simplification, then, to
say that natural-supernatural is a distinction foreign to Bernard, as is said by A. Van den Bosch, 'Présupposée à la chris-

tologie bernardine,' *Citeaux in de Nederlanden* 9 (1958) 5-17, 85-105, at p. 5.

46. Dil VIII, 23.

47. Cf. 1 Cor 15:46, Dil VIII, 23.

48. Dil VIII, 23.

49. Dil X, 27.

50. SC 80.2.

51. Christine Mohrmann, 'Observations sur la langue et le style de saint Bernard,' SBOp II:xx, notes that love in the Sermons is Origen's *eros* rather than the traditional *diligere*, though *deligere* remains the normal expression.

52. SC 79.1.

53. SC 20.9: 'Bonus tamen amor iste carnalis...Proficitur autem in eo, cum sit et rationalis [cf. fidei ratio]; perficitur cum efficitur etiam spiritualis.'

54. Corneille Halflants, 'Le Cantique des cantiques de saint Bernard,' *Collectanea* 15(1953) 274: 'Il ne croit pas qu'il soit possible de comprimer impunément cette force incoercible qu'est l'amour passion.' Henri de Lubac, *Exégèse médiévale*, 4 vols. (Paris, 1959-64) II: 408, notices in other medieval writers an intermediate sense which is merely 'a sort of parenthesis.'

55. Anders Nygren, *Agape and Eros*, trans., Philip S. Wetson (Philadelphis, 1953) p. 650. Nygren here generalizes upon the notions of St Bernard (pp. 645-48) and Aquinas (pp. 642-45) on unselfish love for God. He proposes instead a Lutheran concept of complete discontinuity between the action of grace (*Agape*) and human love (*eros*). Nygren does indeed understand the persistence of human love in Bernard's conception of the love of God. He fails however to see Bernard's idea of how the *affectiones* relate to the action of grace. In generalizing upon the era, he claims its mysticism 'attacks not only selfishness, but selfhood' (p. 650). This conception of the union of the self and God is foreign to Bernard, who repeats that union with God is not a fusion of natures, but a conformity of wills (for example, SC 83.3). Bernard's mystical aspiration is not the loss of self, but a holding of all in common as with spouses, particularly the common will (for example, SC 7.2).

56. SC 44.4: 'Ex intimis sane humanis affectibus primordia ducit sui ortus fraterna dilectio et de insita homini ad seipsum naturali quadam dulcedine tamquam de humore terreno, sumit procul dubio **vegetationem et vim** per quam, spirante quidem gratia desuper, fructus parturit pietatis, ut quod sibi anima naturaliter appetit, naturae consorti, id est alteri homini, iure quodam humanitatis, ubi poterit et oportuerit, non aestimet denegandum, sed sponte ac libens impertiat. Inest ergo naturae, si peccato non obsolescat, istiusmodi gratae et egregiae quasi suavitatis liquor, ut molliorem magis ad compatiendum peccantibus quam ad indignamdam asperiorem se sentiat.'

57. SC 20.8: '**Licet** vero donum et magnum donum Spiritus sit istiusmodi erga carnem Christi devotio, carnalem tamen dixerim hunc amorem, illius utique amoris respectu, quo non tam Verbum caro iam sapit quam Verbum sapientia.'

58. SC 25.8, 28.11, 47.6.

59. SC 20.6.

60. SC 20.6, 6.3.

61. J.-Ch. Didier, 'La dévotion à l'humanité du Christ dans la spiritualité de saint Bernard,' (n. 1 above), offers several criticisms like the following: 'Il n'a pas autant insisté--ni, peut-être, autant saisi par elle--sur la grande réalité toujours actuelle qu'est pour le chrétien le Christ glorieux, chef du **corps** mystique, et sur le mystère de la vie de Jesu' (p. 6). In SC 20, Didier's reference, the **touching** vignettes on the life of Christ are part of a structure leading to 20.7-9, which develops the notion, 'Spiritus ante faciem nostram Christus Dominus'--the actual reality of Christ. Again, 'Mais jamais notre saint n'insiste alors sur cette unité de vie qui fait du chrétien un même être mystique avec le Christ' (p. 6). The precise opposite is true, and states the central subject of every sermon in the Sermons. Didier is able to bring to his support E. Mâle, *L'Art religieux de la fin du moyen âge en France* (Paris, 1922) p. 28; and P. Pourrat, *La Spiritualité chrétienne* (Paris, 1921) p. 38; II, 31. Gilson's vigorous objections (1932) to Pourrat's view of bernardine theology opened an era of study on Bernard. *The Mystical Theology of Saint Bernard* gives an exposition of the system which Pourrat imagined lacking (see pp. vii-viii on Pourrat). Mâle's work is celebrated as a study of religious art; it has not been proposed as an analysis of mystical theology.

In explanation of Bernard's 'devotion' to the humanity of
Christ are A. Van den Bosch, in many articles—for example, 'Le
Christ, Dieu devenu imitable d'après S. Bernard,' *Collectanea*
22 (1960) 341-55; Halflants, pp. 272-76; Knotzinger, p. 36;
and J. Leclercq, *S. Bernard et l'esprit cistercien* (Paris, 1966)
pp. 94, 96. [*Bernard of Clairvaux and the Cistercian Spirit*,
CS 16].

62. SC 20.7, cf. Jn 6:64.

63. SC 20.9.

BERNARDIAN IDEAS IN WOLFRAM'S *PARZIVAL*
ABOUT CHRISTIAN WAR AND HUMAN DEVELOPMENT

JOHN H. CLELAND

Many good critics agree that the *Parzival* of Wolfram von Eschenbach raised the 'matter of Britain,' or arthurian legend, to
its highest peak of literary craftsmanship. This achievement is
all the more remarkable in light of the splendid peaks to which
that craftsmanship occasionally rose during the three hundred-
year period between the mid-twelfth and mid-fifteenth centuries--
and to which it rose once again in the nineteenth and twentieth
centuries. During the medieval period alone, English, French, and
two major German authors other than Wolfram created masterpieces
out of the great fund of arthurian materials. At least four of
these medieval works are to this day considered monumental achieve-
ments in world literature.[1]

What I wish to demonstrate here is the manifest influence of
St Bernard of Clairvaux on Wolfram's masterwork. It is, I think,
this influence that explains the work's universality and surpass-
ing power. I believe that two bernardian ideas in particular were
shaped by Wolfram to constitute the synthetic, formal principle of
Parzival--or plot, in aristotelian poetic theory, that holds everything together--and that this primary internal cause of effects
gives meaning to the action, depth to the character, and power of
the work as a whole.

Other arthurian writers in medieval and modern times have
constructed excellent chivalric romances out of such traditions
as Arthur's great personal prowess in battle, the enterprising
nature of his celtic kingship culminating in the successful defi-
ance of Imperial Rome, the marvellous adventures and romantic
loves of Arthur's knights, and the strangely beautiful Grail quest.
Wolfram's story easily equals the best of them as a tale of the
remote, the exotic, and all the exaggerated aspects of what has
been called the 'Golden Age of Chivalry.' The bavarian writer's
long narrative poem, however, goes beyond chivalric romance as it
is usually understood. It achieves true epic amplitude, for example, in terms of the formulation of E. M. W. Tillyard, by which
four notes of the epic spirit are to be found: a high, distinguished style, which Wolfram achieves even while giving full vent
to his comic spirit; an ample, broad, and inclusive subject matter
that takes for its ideal 'the whole truth'; sustained concentration and powerful predetermined control based on multiple principles of organization; and a choric nature in which the writer expresses the feelings of a large group of people living in or near

his own time, and thus bears personal witness to their system of beliefs or way of life.[2]

Wolfram's epic is especially rich in its presentation of 'the whole truth.' In particular, as Margaret Fitzgerald Richey states,

> the legend of the Grail, with which the Arthurian legend
> is interwoven, assumes in Wolfram's epic such full sig-
> nificance that it claims to be considered alone. The
> realm of King Arthur and the realm of the Grail are two
> distinct though interacting spheres, and the hero Par-
> zival has a place in them both. But he belongs more
> positively to the latter. Despite his membership of
> the Table Round, he is never more than a guest at King
> Arthur's court, here today and gone tomorrow. His des-
> tined heritage is Munsalvaesche: it is there that his
> appointed goal is set.[3]

It is on the epic note of sustained concentration and powerful predetermined control, however, that this examination will focus. As readers of *Parzival* know, the poem contains a bewildering and seemingly unruly wealth of incident. Wolfram's tone showed that he reveled in performing his self-assigned task of telling 'the whole truth' about a vast and peculiar body of celtic legends whose appeal will evidently live on as long as western civilization lasts. At the same time, unifying this enormous amount of detail requires an especially rigorous organization, which is the point where Bernard's reformulation of the germanic warrior ethic and his particularly insightful theory about internal human growth were applied by his near-contemporary, Wolfram von Eschenbach.

Wolfram calls special attention to these two ideas when, in the poem's prologue, he hails his hero as brave, or bold (*küenne*), and slowly wise *(trâclîche wîs)*.[4] All through his poem, Wolfram holds up for admiration many values, but none does he hold as high as knightly valor and wisdom concerning divine matters. The author employs Arthur's Round Table, and particularly Parzival's friend Gawan, as preeminent expressions, along with Parzival himself, of the sort of knightly courage that pleases God; but rising even a-bove these expressions of the warrior ethic is that of the knights who guard the mysterious kingdom of the Grail. And to reach this kingdom, which lies beyond the earthly nobility of the arthurian circle, Parzival must pass through successive stages of worldly glory and shame, gradually maturing in spirit until he is fit to attain his goal and birthright--as King of the Holy Grail.

In the matter of knightly courage, Bernard of Clairvaux de-lineated the most perfect figure of chivalric manhood as conceived by the Middle Ages, an ideal that Jean Leclercq has called the

soldier-monk.[5] To do this, Bernard synthesized in the soul of a
christian knight two characteristics that in modern thought ex-
clude each other: a pure life style and spiritual meekness, on
one hand; on the other an application of fierce military force in
defense of the fatherland, by which Bernard meant Christendom.[6]
The saint had historical models to draw on when he fashioned this
unusual synthesis, and it is also true that the Templars of history
had been in existence for ten years before Bernard set out to make
them into soldier-monks. But Bernard it was who precisely formulated the balance between physical force and spiritual ideal in
those historical knights who obviously served as models for Wolfram's Grail knights. Bernard subjected force to spirit in the
Templars but with no dimunition of the force. He more than anyone else tamed the lion at the core of the germanic warrior ethic;
but he did this, in Chesterton's happy phrase, without making it
lamb-like.

     The other and even more important bernardian idea we find ap-
plied in Wolfram's epic involves an equally original balancing of
opposed tendencies. I refer to Bernard's theory about the painful
gradualness of human growth in knowledge and wisdom and unselfish
love of God and neighbor. Other christian thinkers, especially
the Greek Fathers, have dwelt on the two conditions of human nature postulated by orthodox Christianity: the condition of man as
he was created (good, in the image and likeness of God, with a
natural yearning for God, and with a natural capability of return-
ing to God); and the condition of man as he has existed since the
Fall (turned away from God towards self, blocked off from the natural avenue of return). But here again, no one has created a
more startling though plausible fusion of these two human aspects
than Bernard was able to create. He emphasized each aspect at its
full power. He taught that a man begins to recapture his true
created nobility when he comes to recognize, in the depths of humiliation, the true extent of his moral deformity.[7] Humility becomes for Bernard the only mediating agent between the deformity
and nobility of man, the great psychological pre-condition for
genuine growth in knowledge and unselfish love. And he further
taught that this growth is typically very slow.[8]

     The controlled and deliberate evolution of Parzival's char-
acter has been much admired by Wolfram scholars. Otto Springer,
for example, calls attention to the almost complete absence of
this writing technique in the other medieval stories of chivalry
and suggests it as the technique that enabled Wolfram to bring order out of so much otherwise chaotic detail. For Parzival's experiences, says Springer,

     no longer take their own more or less accidental
     course but represent successive phases of the

hero's metamorphosis.[9]

But if Wolfram drew on bernardian psychology in order to show the evolution of his hero's character, he also drew on a related strand of Bernard's thought, an epistemology based on acquiring knowledge through the senses and not through mystical neo-platonic insights. One way for a fiction writer to delay the formation of character is to delay the introduction of knowledge on which that character is formed, and especially to delay the introduction of teachers who can impart character-forming knowledge. This is what Wolfram does; he makes Parzival learn just as the rest of us are forced to learn, through character-forming teachers encountered over long periods. And if it seems to some that so great an author as Wolfram would not need an epistemological theory, from Bernard or anyone else, in order to embed this rather basic truth into imaginative literature, I would ask them why so few other great medieval writers before Dante were able to show the stages of an evolving character.

Another reason for the structural complexity of *Parzival*, I believe, was Wolfram's intention of realistically depicting the educative aspect of a whole society; in other words how that society and, in particular, its most effective schoolmasters in life were able to educate Parzival. Relating the matter again to real life, where our most effective schoolmasters do not appear one after the other between birth and puberty, this would explain how Wolfram was able in practice to portray a gradual maturation process. For whether or not the German poet learned his epistemology from Bernard, he knew that men acquire their knowledge not as angels do, with immediate intuitive force and penetration, but rather through the senses, slowly, only with the help of teachers, and normally in the school of experience.

In a useful overview of the intersecting story lines of the narrative, Wolfram scholar Hugh Sacker brings together the poet's dual emphasis on the nobility of the knightly ethic, even one less exalted than Bernard's, and on the hero's struggle for a wisdom that transcends worldly wisdom. Sacker writes:

> Wolfram's *Parzival* contains the stories of three men: the titular hero, his father, and his friend...all three men are knights, and the work is primarily concerned with the possibilities of life open to a knight; the other professions play little part in the story, though hermits are of some importance, since a knight --or lady--can forsake the special position to which he was born and devote himself to God...none of the three men ever consciously betrays the code of chivalry; they always do their best, and the trials which

come their way are not those which beset a man who
deliberately turns to evil, but those which over-
take the best-intentioned of men.

The three are distinguished from each other according to their potentialities and their fate: Gahmuret
[Parzival's father] is an independent adventurer who
can never resist the call of battle or love and dies
young...Gawan [Parzival's friend] is a leading member
of society, a knight of the Round Table who is both
sensible and valiant and who, after resolving a number of his society's vexed questions, marries and
may be presumed to settle down; Parzival inherits his
father's reckless drive, early acquires membership of
the Round Table and the happiness of a perfect mar-
riage--and then discovers to his dismay that for him
this is not enough. He is ignorant that through his
mother's family he is called to higher things--in
which for obscure reasons of inheritance and upbringing he fails--and is cursed in public by a messenger
from the mysterious Grail. There follow four and a
half years of misery and isolation, then an investigation of spiritual truth and of the values and con-
stitution of the Grail--to which he is eventually
called with his wife and one son when he is fit to
be its king.[10]

Sacker then suggests a social dimension of the story that goes
beyond the exploits of its titular hero:

The work as a whole is thus not simply concerned with
an exceptional man, though it does present his problems with subtlety, insight, and conviction, but also
with his relationship to other types of men and to
society in general. Those who concentrate, as many
have done, on the story of the main hero, miss this
wider significance.[11]

In other words, we find in the medieval Christendom Wolfram portrays
a vital tension between the singularity of one man's course and the
solidarity that unites him to others and in the end fecundates his
personal achievement.

Wolfram does dramatize one man in a multitude. He represents
his hero's vehement longing for personal glory as consciously, and
with as much authorial fervor, as Homer represented this traditional mainspring of the warrior ethic. He expands the possibilities
of the perfect homeric knight, of course, with a Christianity that

includes eternal as well as temporal glory. The author's praise
for this desire never slackens. At one point he says that Parzival

> felt that noble striving was a lofty goal both in
> this life and the next. And that is still no lie. (177)

But Wolfram also dramatizes the multitude and especially, as
I have claimed, the teaching function of that vast assortment of
characters. J. G. Robertson aptly described the German poet's
mastery of character delineation when he said of the work:

> No other epic of chivalry presents so varied a picture
> or is so rich in living creations, in men and women who,
> after a lapse of seven centuries, are still so humanly
> interesting.[12]

Many of these living creations impart knowledge to Parzival
that turns out to be useless or worse. Prominent among those who
transmit important knowledge to him are Prince Gurnemanz de Gra-
harz, the wise old man who teaches the young man chivalric ways.
But it is two recluses, Parzival's cousin Sigune and the hermit
Trevrizent, who impart to him the most important teachings he ever
receives. Sigune first reveals to Parzival his name, helps him
discover who he is psychologically, and tells him what he finally
must do at Munsalvaesche in order to merit his birthright there.

When Parzival encounters Trevrizent for the first time, in
the ninth of Wolfram's sixteen books, we begin to encounter Bernard's explicit influence on the work. And Book IX is also generally acknowledged to be the artistic center of the poem, its 'very
core' in the opinion of Otto Springer.[13]

Parzival's situation prior to meeting Trevrizent must be grasp-
ed in order to appreciate the bernardian echoes of that interview.
Parzival's four and a half years of misery and isolation, alluded
to earlier, began with a series of misfortunes attributable more to
his ignorance than to any malice in him. He spent the ensuing years
wandering through the world: at war with God, whom he misunderstood
as a remote feudal lord whose hand might be forced through services
rendered; deliberately separated from the wife he loved and remained
true to; at war with himself, doubting, fighting, seeking; and most
of all filled with a deep longing to recover the transcendent value
he knew to be associated with the Grail but about which he had no
clear knowledge. And though he had kept his physical courage intact throughout the whole period, his heart had become progressively hardened against the very God whose help he sought in his quest.

We know from Bernard's writings that on more than one occasion
he opened his mind publicly with highly revealing admissions about

his own passionate nature. In one place he says:

> I am not ashamed to admit that very often I myself,
> especially in the early days of my conversion, experi-
> enced coldness and hardness of heart, while deep in my
> being I sought for him who I longed to love. I could
> not yet love him since I had not yet really found him;
> at best my love was less than it should have been, and
> for that very reason I sought to increase it, for I
> would not have sought him if I did not love him in some
> degree.[14]

Parzival is finally led to Trevrizent on a Good Friday morning.
The ground covered with a thin coating of snow, Parzival meets some
pilgrims in the forest, an old knight with his wife and daughters.
The knight reproaches Parzival for bearing arms on so holy a day.
But Parzival knows nothing of holy days; in matters of religious
observance, he is still a simpleton. The old man then begs him to
seek out a hermit who lives in the forest, and to free himself from
his load of sin.

The bernardian passage quoted above continues:

> I sought him therefore that in him my numbed and
> languid spirit might find warmth and repose, for
> nowhere could I find a friend to help me, whose
> love would thaw the wintry cold that chilled my in-
> ward being, and bring back again the feeling of
> spring-like bliss and spiritual delight. But my
> languor and weariness only increased, my soul melt-
> ed away for sorrow, even to the verge of despair.
> All I could do was repeat softly to myself: 'Who
> can stand before his cold?' Then, at times when I
> least expected, at the word or even the sight of a
> good and holy man, at the memory of a dead or absent
> friend, he set his wind blowing and the waters flow-
> ing, and my tears were my food day and night. How
> can I explain this? Only by ascribing it to the
> odor from the oil that annointed the friend in
> question. For me there was no annointing, but
> rather the experience that came by another's medi-
> ation.[15]

Repentence begins to steal into Parzival's soul as he decides
to take the stranger's advice and find the hermit. He lets his
horse wander where it will, saying that if God is really so mighty
he will guide it. The horse brings him to Trevrizent, who turns
out to be the brother of the wounded Grail king and Parzival's own

deceased mother. But before learning about these family ties, Parzival presents himself to the hermit with the simple words: 'Sir, now give me counsel. I am a man who has sinned.' (456)

What we can discover first of all from the Trevrizent interview is Parzival beginning to attain a depth of feeling that he had so notably lacked in his first meeting with the wounded Grail king, when he had not asked the one simple compassionate question of the king--'Sir, why is it that you suffer so?'--that would have spiritually equipped Parzival to learn, then and there, the true nature of the Grail.

While it is true that Wolfram would not have needed the bernardian text quoted above as the basis for his 'Parzival and Trevrizent' chapter IX--one apparently had no need to travel far in the Germany of 1200, to encounter large numbers of benign strangers and holy recluses living on the outskirts of populated areas--the resemblance in tone between the two descriptions of spiritual conversion is remarkable. I would also remark the tonal resemblance between Bernard and Trevrizent in the succeeding stages of that poetic interview. For Trevrizent's style, too, reveals strong traces of the attractively human qualities in Bernard that so impressed his medieval contemporaries--from the hermit's boyish enthusiasm for the Grail knights to the way he paints, with a fine black bernardian brush, each sin he drags out of his nephew.

It is in the literal content of Trevrizent's instruction, however, that Wolfram's reliance upon bernardian formulations becomes most apparent. The hermit's words about the Grail knights--'Blessed is the mother who bore a child to do service there' (471)--ring for example with the same idealism and pride Bernard showered for more than two decades on the Order of the Temple.

Trevrizent goes on to explain how very far removed the ideals of this Grail knighthood are from the unrestrained pride and violence and courtly love that foolish worldly knights honor.

> Such ways are not fitting for the Grail. There both
> knight and squire must guard themselves against in-
> continence. Humility has conquered their pride. A
> noble brotherhood dwells there, who with valiant
> strength have warded off the people of all lands so
> that the Grail is unknown save to those who have
> been called by name to Munsalvaesche to the Grail's
> company. (473)

Trevrizent also explains that all the Grail knights with the single exception of their lord remain celibate, and that they must occasionally undertake secret missions to other lands, sometimes to rule God-fearing peoples who have lost their previous lords and who seek replacements from among the Grail company.

Bernard's authorship of the rule for the Order of the Temple, in 1128, is undisputed--and we can surely conclude that it and the exhortatory sermon the saint subsequently addressed to the master of the Templars, the public letter entitled *In Praise of the New Knighthood*, were as well known in the Christendom of 1200 as they are now. Bernard in that letter described the vain excesses of worldly chivalry:

> What, therefore, is the purpose or the fruit of this worldly--I cannot call it a militia but a malice--if the killer sins fatally, and the one killed eternally perishes?...Therefore, O knights, what astounding error is this, what insupportable madness is here, to fight with much expenses and such efforts for no pay at all, unless it be death or crime? You cover your horses with silk cloths; you place over your cuirasses hangings of I know not what material; you paint your lances, shields, and saddles; you embellish your reins and your spurs with gold, silver, and gems. With such pomp, in shameful furor and thoughtless stupor you hurry to your deaths. Are these the ornaments of soldiers, or rather women? Will perchance the enemy's sword respect the gold, spare the gems, and be unable to penetrate the silks?[16]

The mordant irony here must surely have appealed to so vigorous a writer as Wolfram, even though his respect for chivalric trappings was greater than Bernard's. And he may also have remembered the satirical thrust of the passage, if not the very words, when he decided to have the very young and uncouth Parzival kill his own kinsman, whom he did not know to be that, for a suit of red armor.

Bernard concluded the first part of his exhortation with a brief discussion of the morals and lifestyle of the Templars:

> Both in food and garments all excess is avoided, and only necessity is considered. They live in common, in a cheerful and sober manner, without wives and without children...they keep no private possession, but they live as a single community in a single house...in the entire throng there is but a single heart and a single soul...they are attentive to one another in honor; they bear one another's burdens, so that they may fulfill the law of Christ. Insolent speech, useless actions, immoderate laughter, even a low grumble or whisper never, when they are noticed, are left unpunished.[17]

The sadness at Munsalvaesche does not exactly match the sobriety Bernard recommends to the Templars, but the living style there
matches his model in more important ways than the transient mood
of the place. It exhibits a complete unity of purpose, a dignified
gravity, a fellow-feeling for the wounded king, and no apparent sexual activity or normal family life despite the fact of its hetero-
sexual character.

Above all, the contemplative atmosphere of castle life at Munsalvaesche, which is analogous to what Bernard considers at great
length in the second part of his treatise on Christian chivalry as
exemplified by the Templars, exactly matches that of Bernard's ideal
men outside monastery walls. The point of the treatise to the Templars, according to Leclercq,

> is that it relativizes the military profession and links
> it up with a prayer life, even giving prayer the first
> place. The purpose of the militia is not only war but
> prayer as well.[18]

And at Munsalvaesche, the hermit explains to his nephew Parzival,
life revolves around ceremonies associated with the Grail.

Many analysts of *Parzival* have commented on Wolfram's rather
obvious use of the Templars as the general model for his Grail
knights. Without at all disputing this, it seems inescapable to me
that the man who articulated the Templars' ideals and effectively
circulated those ideals throughout Christendom should be considered
the true source of Wolfram's ideas about Christian chivalry at its
highest pitch.

When we consider Bernard's very elaborately developed program-
matic doctrine of internal human growth in knowledge and love, a
doctrine he returns to regularly in most of his treatises, and especially in the *Song of Songs*, and *On Loving God*,[19] Wolfram's cre-
ative debt to the obviously kindred spirit who died just two genera-
tions before he began writing begins to appear enormous. Before examining this network of relationships, however, a question needs to
be asked. What access to Bernard's written work could Wolfram like-
ly have had? Without even pausing to consider the German poet's ec-
centrically humorous claim to being illiterate, except to mention it,
we know first of all that there was an immense circulation and dili-
gent transcription of Bernard's works during and following the saint's
own lifetime. One of his twentieth century biographers cites in support of the contemporary influence of Bernard's written works--thir-
teen treatises, about 350 sermons, and upwards of 500 letters--the
testimony of Bernard's doctrinal enemy Berengarius.[20] We can also
be sure that the cistercian monasteries throughout Europe served as
transmission belts for the works--and there were about 350 cistercian houses at the time of Bernard's death in 1153.

According to one of the recent medieval library catalogue editions of the combined German Academies of Munich, *Mittelalterliche Bibliothekskataloge*, numerous bernardian manuscripts were housed in libraries at Passau by the year 1200. According to the cataloguer of the medieval libraries of the bishopric of Passau, a town on the Danube now at the German-Austrian border, Wolfram was a member of the court literary circle and therefore had access to manuscripts owned by the court. Those manuscripts, according to the Munich catalogue, included sermons and letters of Bernard, *On Consideration*, and works of 'blessed Bernard.'[21] Wolfram is believed to have begun writing *Parzival* around 1197 or 1198.

The gaping spiritual, intellectual, and psychological voids in the young hero of the story turn out to be the very same ones Bernard labored a lifetime to fill up in himself and to help his fellow men fill up in themselves. The author's prominently claimed emphasis on the gradualness of Parzival's inner growth was a theme Bernard never tired of treating. Early in his eighty-six sermons on the *Song of Songs*, he says:

> I do not wish to be suddenly on the heights, my desire
> is to advance by degrees. The impudence of the sinner
> displeases God as much as the modesty of the penitent
> gives him pleasure. You will please him more readily
> if you live within the limits proper to you, and do
> not set your sights at things beyond you. It is a
> long and formidable leap from the foot to the mouth,
> a manner of approach that is not commendable. Con-
> sider for a moment: still tarnished as you are with
> the dust of sin, would you dare touch those sacred
> lips? Yesterday you were lifted from the mud, today
> you wish to encounter the glory of his face? No, his
> hand must be your guide to that end. First it must
> cleanse your stains, then it must raise you up. How
> raise you? *By giving you the grace to dare to aspire.*[22]

Bernard's theory of knowledge, which he grounded on the senses being the great ordinary means by which men come to know truth, also emerges strongly in the development of Parzival. When Trevrizent learns that his nephew is the man who could have relieved the sadness of the Grail company--by being the one who asks the wounded Grail king the sensible and compassionate question mentioned earlier--the hermit says this:

> God gave you five senses, but they denied you their aid.
> How did they help you then, at the wound of Anfortas,
> to preserve your loyalty? (488)

In his fifth sermon on the *Song of Songs*, Bernard contrasts
the way men and angels arrive at truth. The latter, he says, can
soar to the highest truths and penetrate their profoundest depths
by means of the vital force and kinship of their nature. But with
man things are different.

> St Paul implied this when he said: 'The invisible
> things of God are understood through the things he
> has made,' adding the qualification, 'by the creature
> of the world' [Romans 1:20]. Because this is not so
> for the creature of heaven. For, what the spirit
> clothed in flesh and dwelling on the earth strives
> to achieve *gradually and little by little,* through
> the knowledge it derives from the senses, that same
> dweller of the heavens attains with all speed and
> ease, because of the native fineness and sublime
> quality of its being.[23]

Bernard wanted man to dare to aspire to temporal glory as
well as spiritual glory, when and if a field of action necessitated
doing great things in this world. When preaching the Second Crusade, he consistently appealed to the pride of the kings and nobles
to do their duty, gloriously, for European Christendom. But both
he and Wolfram stressed that such glory-seeking must be accomplished
within the realistic limits of human nature. Both writers focus on
the contrasting negative and positive aspects of chivalry, as a system of life, and present an ideal difficult to attain but for that
reason extraordinarily bracing. They are not like the detractors of
chivalry who content themselves to point only to its besetting sins
of vainglory and excess. They both do that, but they both also
point to the potential greatness of noble chivalric action. Trevrizent, for example, does not deny the following words that Parzival
says to him:

> If knighthood with shield and spear can win renown in
> this life and Paradise for the soul as well--for knight-
> hood I have always striven. I fought wherever I found
> a battle, and in such way that my armed hand had high-
> est honor within its reach. If God is a good judge of
> fighting, he should summon me by name to the Grail so
> that they may come to know me. My hand shall not fail
> me there in battle. (472)

Trevrizent simply answers that this is not enough, that humility
and self-discipline and temperance are needed in addition to prowess and courage and the strong sense of natural justice he knows
Parzival already possesses. And he warns Parzival of the great

besetting sin of chivalric pride, which has been so disastrously
punished in the life of the wounded Grail king, Anfortas. Springer
calls the hermit's emphasis on humility the *leit-motif* of his teaching to Parzival, and points to the recurring character of the virtue throughout Wolfram's entire book.[24]

But in my opinion Trevrizent performs his greatest educational
service to the young knight by imparting to him a sense of creature-
hood and an ultimate dependence on God's goodness for his prowess
in battle, his talents, and for his very life. Hugh Sacker touches
on these great deficiencies in self-knowledge, which amount to much
more than a mere lack of information about religious observance or
theology in Parzival, when he says:

> ...ignorant as he is of original sin, of which so far as
> we know no mention has yet been made to him by anyone,
> Parzival declines to take upon himself full responsibility
> for his failure at Munsalvaesche....Of the unpayable debt
> man owes to God on account of Adam's first sin--which
> Parzival has inherited--and of God's limitless goodness
> in redeeming his debtor on the Cross, the young knight
> knows nothing. Nor is he, in his self-centeredness, will-
> ing to learn; he assumes he is right and God wrong, and
> that if he only persists in his course he must triumph.
> Such self-righteousness is in strong contrast to Parzival's
> sense of shame; he knows that he has failed in his ap-
> pointed task and is ashamed but, ignorant of the reasons
> for failure, he refuses stubbornly to admit that the
> fault is his. It takes four and a half years of misery
> ...to break his obstinacy and make him ready to learn.
> Disgrace and failure are needed to bring Parzival, the
> child of Adam, back to God.[25]

In Bernard's thought, a man cannot know God until he knows himself.

> See, then, in what a miserable and accursed condition
> a man is who is found in ignorance of God. Ignorance
> of God, or of his own self, ought I to say? Unquestion-
> ably both the one and the other--each kind of ignorance
> is fatal, and each suffices to bring about everlasting
> perdition. Would you know how this is the case? As re-
> gards ignorance of God, you will, I think, have no doubt,
> if you believe without question that this only is eternal
> life, to know the true God, and Jesus Christ whom He has
> sent [John 15:3]. Listen, then, to the Bridegroom, who
> condemns clearly and unmistakably in the soul   ignor-
> ance of itself. For what does he say? Not, 'if you know

not God,' but 'if you know not yourself, etc. [Cant. 1:7].'[26]

Wolfram thus follows the original emphasis Bernard placed not only on the benefits of humility as the crowning quality of Christian chivalry. At an even deeper psychological level, he like Bernard recognizes the specifically intellectual benefits of the quality. Humility seems to be one of those virtues that Christians and nearly everyone else have always given lip service to but have only vaguely understood. Why did Wolfram emphasize it so? Bernard once again adds the precision needed to understand the exact way Wolfram links up humility with self-knowledge, when in the *Song of Songs* he says:

> I wish therefore that before everything a man should know himself, because not only usefulness but right order demand this. Right order, since what we are is our first concern; and usefulness, because this knowledge gives humility rather than self-importance, *it provides a basis on which to build.* For unless there is a durable foundation of humility, the spiritual edifice has no hope of standing. And there is nothing more effective, more adapted to the acquiring of humility, than to find out the truth about oneself. There must be no dissimulation, no attempt at self-deception, but a facing up to one's real self without flinching and turning aside. When a man thus takes stock of himself in the clear light of truth, he will discover that he lives in a region where likeness to God has been forfeited, and groaning from the depths of a misery to which he can no longer remain blind, will he not cry out to the Lord as the Prophet did: 'In your truth you have humbled me?'[27]

Parzival's chief problem right along has gone deeper than his abysmal ignorance. He has not really learned the truth about himself or about anything else of consequence because he has never really wanted to learn the truth. In his unjustified self-righteousness, he believed he did not need to. We see a man at last admit, in the presence of the benign but sharp-tongued Trevrizent, that he does not know everything. And thus we see him at last begin to learn something. His confession is more than vaguely edifying.

It is in the 'Parzival and Trevrizent' chapter, then, that the hero begins his sharpest ascent to true wisdom. For it is there that Wolfram successfully applied the widely known, rarely enough achieved, and generally misunderstood teaching of Jesus about the inherent connection between humility and human glory: that men must detach themselves from the world's purely secular influences, and very often mistaken admirations, in order to achieve true mastery

of their own fortunes; that if we humble ourselves we will be exalted.

Christ was referring to exaltation in the life to come. That
he did not rule out the possibility of ethically valid glory in the
temporal order may be understood on a variety of scriptural grounds,
however,[28] and not the least of these grounds are the ones Bernard
cites in his sermon to the Templars as reasons for physically de-
fending the Christian holy places associated with Jerusalem, 'the
city of the Lord of hosts' as Bernard calls it, quoting the forty-
eighth psalm. He continues:

> Of course this literal interpretation, which we have
> applied from the words of the prophets to our own times,
> ought not to prejudice spiritual meanings, by which we
> are led to hope in eternity. Otherwise, that which is
> seen will erase that which is believed, and an impover-
> ished reality may diminish the riches of hope; the ex-
> perience of present things would be a loss of things to
> come. Rather *the temporal glory of the earthly city*
> does not diminish the good things of heaven, but adds to
> them, if only we do not hesitate to consider this city
> a figure of our mother who is in heaven.[29]

In the great assigned role Parzival was called upon to play in
this world, as King of the Holy Grail, his literary creator had to
deal once again with the age-old question of finding an equilibrium
between pride and humility. He seems to have found such an equilibrium, and the modern English writer G. K. Chesterton helps us understand the elements that went into Wolfram's solution. According to
Chesterton, orthodox Christianity does not produce an amalgam, or
compromise, between such 'furious opposites' as 'mere pride' and
'mere prostration.' Such an amalgam is what others produce.

> The average pagan, like the average agnostic, would
> merely say that he was content with himself, but not
> insolently self-satisfied, that there were many better
> and many worse, that his deserts were limited, but he
> would see that he got them. In short, he would walk
> with his head in the air; but not necessarily with his
> nose in the air. This is a manly and rational position....[30]

But Chesterton then characterizes that position as so diluted in
both of its aspects that it is not really satisfactory by human
standards; it is neither proud enough nor humble enough.

> This proper pride does not lift the heart like the
> tongue of trumpets; you cannot go clad in crimson

and gold for this. On the other hand, this mild
rationalist modesty does not cleanse the soul with
fire and make it clear like crystal; it does not
(like a strict and searching humility) make a man as
a child, who can sit at the feet of the grass. It
does not make him look up and see marvels; for Alice
must grow small if she is to be Alice in Wonderland.
Thus it loses both the poetry of being proud and the
poetry of being humble.[31]

    Wolfram's muscular Christian faith enabled him to save both
kinds of poetry. I referred earlier in this examination of Bernard's
influence on the composition of *Parzival* to Wolfram's balancing of
opposed tendencies. Such a balance certainly appears in the poetry
of pride and that of humility. Both are discoverable in *Parzival*.
Both are 'burning,' in another chestertonian phrase.
    The pride is a pride, mainly, in physical prowess and courage
in war or single combat--the heroic ethic classically expressed.
But more than other chivalric writers, Wolfram transforms the glory-
seeking motives of these bloody encounters to ethically superior,
defense-minded motives; the motives, in short, of the Grail knighthood. This really amounts to a revaluation of the use of brute
force, and for Wolfram as for Bernard the transformation takes place
in the name of Christ. It perhaps is not stretching the point to
call that revaluation a christianization of war.[32]
    But if the pride is essentially a martial pride, the other
bernardian influence I have found in *Parzival* is essentially a
striving towards a peaceful spirit, and one that is born of a
warrior's checkmated pride in himself and his own resources of
prowess and courage. Parzival has found those resources incapable
of helping him achieve, unaided, what he most wants to achieve, the
Grail. Wolfram thus dramatizes the insufficiency of even a noble
chivalry in the very same way Bernard shortly before him had drama-
tized it: by showing that the ultimately successful way a man finds
God is by searching inside himself, not by sailing across the seas,
or rising up into the clouds, or crossing the mountains.
    The heroic christianized ethic of Wolfram's *Parzival* signifies
why arthurian and bernardian chivalry will remain forever green.
And it will remain so despite the contrary judgment of those modern
readers who are not thrilled by the early heroic poetry of their
race. But that ethic, transformed by Christian standards of right
and wrong, and held high above western lances as the banner of the
mystery of chivalry, will also resist ethical corruption by such
false would-be continuators as Wagner and Hitler. The Christian
motives of Wolfram's hero cannot be transmuted, as Wagner tried to
do in his opera, into a mere dream of beauty or the vital impulses
of the *Volk*. Nor can a Hitler achieve more than momentary and

isolated success with lies aimed at reconstituting a 'heroic conception of life.' For thoughtful Christians know that no human actions are incommensurable with the standard of good and evil set forth by Christ; that there can be no greatness where simplicity, goodness, and truth are absent.

Finally I would suggest, with Georges Cattaui and M.-M. Davy, that there may be a special relationship between Bernard's monastic ideals and Wolfram's symbolic representation of the Grail mysteries.[33] This relationship would appear to go beyond any of the formally stated themes of Bernard's teachings and Wolfram's epic poem, including the theme of achieving true self-understanding through humility. The correspondence I refer to involves the central hope of the christian faith: God's promise to unite the very core of his being, mystically, with that of anyone who first perfects himself through service and sacrifice. We know that Bernard himself dared to aspire to this level of reality, and we know from his *Sermons on the Song of Songs* that he was carefully but pointedly challenging others to do the same. I suggest that what Wolfram was symbolically saying, through the knights and ladies of the Grail company, and certain of his other characters related in spirit to that company, is that Bernard's challenge validly applies outside traditional monastery walls--just as the saint himself had taught. If this is true, Parzival's long and painful search for the Grail represents more than a struggle for the possession of spiritual and celestial knowledge. It would then represent a spiritual thirst for the experience of mystical union with God.

Loyola University, Chicago

NOTES

1. The three most noted works other than Wolfram's are *Perceval*, or the *Conte du Graal*, by Chrétien de Troyes; *Tristan und Isolt*, by Gottfried von Strassburg; and *Le Morte Darthur*, by England's Sir Thomas Mallory. Another very distinguished work is *Gawain and the Green Knight*, written by an anonymous Englishman, probably between 1360 and 1400.

2. E. M. W. Tillyard, *The English Epic and Its Background* (New York: Oxford University Press, 1966) pp. 4-13.

3. Margaret F. Richey, 'The German Contribution to the Matter of Britain,' a paper read a meeting of the Oxford Mediaeval Society in 1948 and published subsequently in *Medium Aevum* (no date).

4. A generally recommended edition is the Lachmann text (*Wolfram von Eschenbach*, 6th ed. by E. Hartle, Berlin, 1952), on which the English prose translation cited in this examination (tr. by H. Mustard and C. Passage, New York, 1961) is based. As one who makes no pretense to being a German scholar, I am also indebted to the Middle High German word list and notes in the Marold selection of courtly epics from Hartman von Aue, Wolfram von Eschenbach, and Gottfried von Strassburg (Leipzig, 1908).

5. Jean Leclercq, 'Saint Bernard's Attitude Toward War,' *Studies in Medieval Cistercian History*, II, ed. J. Sommerfeldt, Cistercian Studies Series No. 24 (Kalamazoo, 1976) p. 25.

6. Political theory as such does not appear in Bernard's writings. Many of the issues he addressed, however, and the crusade issue in particular, delineate his view of the ideal functioning of the political order in twelfth-century Europe: as a commonwealth of christian peoples who could occasionally be expected to act in concert on large public matters touching the spiritual welfare of individual Christians, the honor of God, and the good of the Church. The international scope of Bernard's preaching activities in raising the Second Crusade affords a dramatic example of this view of Christendom. Another example emerges from his treatise *In Praise of the New Knighthood*, in which Bernard is obviously moved by no mere national or regional understanding of Christian interests and obligations. He describes in that treatise the spiritual significance of the Holy Land for all Christians, even those like himself who were never inspired to visit it personally; and at great length he reminds his readers of the belief Christians on pilgrimage had been demonstrating for centuries: that Jerusalem was the preeminent earthly

symbol of their ultimate homeland. On this basis Bernard
justifies the use of physical force to guarantee the right
of innocent passage and free access to places that he obviously considered the common possessions of Christendom.

> 'Let therefore the nations who wish for war be scattered,
> let those be cut down who disturb us. Let all who do in-
> iquity be extirpated from the city of the Lord--those who
> sought to rob the christian peoples of the inestimable
> riches preserved at Jerusalem, to profane holy places and
> to hold in inheritance the sanctuary of the Lord. Let
> both swords held by the faithful be drawn against the
> necks of their enemies, in order to destroy all arrogance
> which extols itself against the science of God which is
> the christian faith.' *In Praise*, p. 293 of *The History
> of Feudalism*, ed. D. Herlihy (New York, 1970).

7. Bernard's sermons *On the Song of Songs*, for example, contain
many references to the innate gloriousness of man, which the
saint always insists, however, is to be attributed in justice
to man's creator. The same sermons contain many other references to the gross ignorance of man when he wrongly regards
himself as the source of his human gifts, especially the gift
of reason. Still other references are made to the sort of
despicable human arrogance by which man seeks to glorify himself for gifts he *knows* come from God. Sermons 13, 24, and
35-37 offer representative examples of Bernard's dual emphasis
on the dignity and baseness of man.

In Sermon 34 we can also see how he employs humility as the
rehabilitating agent in man's moral life: 'Anyone who strives
forward toward the spiritual heights must have a lowly opinion
of himself; because when he is raised above himself he may lose
his grip on himself, unless through true humility, he has a
firm hold on himself. It is only when humility warrants it
that great graces can be obtained, hence the one to be enriched
by them is first humbled by correction that by his humility he
may merit them.' 34:1 *On the Song of Songs II*; CF 7:160-
61.

8. We get some idea of the typical slowness of the moral rehabili-
tation of man, as Bernard conceived of the process, in the saint's
formulation of the four degrees of love a man passes through in
his return to God. First of all, the process is a life-long one.
The physical needs of the flesh, including those commanded by God
in the name of brotherly love, more or less constantly interfere
with the soul's desire to pass wholly into God; and this in turn

prevents the soul from attaining, in this life, the highest
possible degree of its love. (The exceptions to this phenomenon count for nothing in Bernard's theory.)

Even passing from the first degree of love to the second is a
laborious and evidently time-consuming undertaking, as Bernard
described it. 'In truth it is to the end that the creature
should not be in ignorance concerning himself, and thus (which
God forbid) arrogantly claim for himself as his own the benefits of the Creator--that this same Creator in his profound
and saving wisdom wills that man should be vexed by tribulations,
so that, when man sinks and God supports him, while man is set
free by God, God, as is fitting, may be honoured by man.' *On
Loving God*, tr. Watkin Williams (from *St Bernard: The Man and
His Message* [Manchester University Press, 1944] pp. 50-72, esp.
63).

9. Otto Springer, 'Wolfram's Parzival,' *Arthurian Literature in
    the Middle Ages*, ed. R. Loomis (Oxford: Clarendon Press, 1959)
    p. 246.

10. Hugh Sacker, *An Introduction to Wolfram's Parzival* (Cambridge,
    1963) pp. xi-xii.

11. *Ibid.*

12. J. G. Robertson, *A History of German Literature*, 6th ed. by D.
    Reich (Edinburgh: Wm. Blackwood, 1970) p. 84.

13. Springer, p. 247.

14. Bernard, Sermon 14.6, *On the Song of Songs I;* CF 4:102.

15. *Ibid.*, pp. 102-103.

16. Bernard, *In Praise of the New Knighthood*, from *The History of
    Feudalism*, ed. Herlihy, p. 291.

17. *Ibid.*, pp. 294-95.

18. Leclercq, 'Saint Bernard's Attitude,' p. 25. The expression of
    this thought comes from Fr Leclercq's original article draft and
    thus differs slightly from the one published. Leclercq makes
    the interesting observation in footnote 72 of his article, p.
    24, that 'the Templars shared to some extent Cistercian spiritu-
    ality' and that this fact 'helped humanize war.' Then he adds,
    'Once again, Bernard created the theory and even the theology of

an already existing fact: that of knights living a religious
life in the Holy Land.'

19. Sermons 10 and 12 *On the Song,* for example, trace the three
practical stages (contrition, devotion, loving-kindness)
through which a soul entangled in sin returns to God, while
at the same time acquiring a richly attractive consolation
at each stage; Sermon 20 develops the idea of how man's love
is gradually reoriented from carnal to spiritual, from concu-
piscence to charity. Bernard's treatise *On Loving God,* taken
as a whole, presents another program of spiritual movement;
here, man moves by slow degrees from an initial, selfish but
natural love of himself alone to a culminating, wholly dis-
interested love of himself solely for the sake of God.

20. Ailbe J. Luddy, O. Cist., *Life and Teaching of St Bernard*
(Dublin, 1927) p. 68.

21. *Mittelalterliche Bibliothekskataloge,* v. 4, bearbeitet von
Christine Elisabeth Ineichen-Eder (München, 1977). In this
connection, I wish to acknowledge two debts: to Professor
Eder, who brought her manuscript research to my attention at
the 1978 Kalamazoo conference, where I delivered a shorter
and less complete version of this examination; and to the
conference sponsors, who make possible this sort of information pooling.

22. Bernard, Sermon 3.4, *On the Song of Songs I*; CF 4: 18-19
(italics mine).

23. Sermon 5.4; CF 4:27 (italics mine).

24. Springer, p. 234.

25. Sacker, pp. 61-62.

26. Sermon 35 *On the Song of Songs,* from the Mabillon edition of
Bernard's *Life and Works,* v. 4 (1896) pp. 232-33.

27. Bernard, Sermon 36.5, *On the Song of Songs II*; CF 7: 177-8
(italics mine).

28. One of those grounds would seem to be Christ's own investment
special authority in Peter and the other apostles. These men
received no command to belittle their assigned parts, nor even
to shrink from whatever earthly prominence would accrue to them

and those who followed them for carrying through the ambitious plan of evangelizing all nations. They were told to serve the word of God and to serve other men. And they were told *how* to perform that service: in a spirit of humble detachment from every other thing save the deposit of faith.

29. Bernard, *In Praise of the New Chivalry*, p. 294 (italics mine).

30. G. K. Chesterton, *Orthodoxy* (Image Books, 1959) p. 93.

31. *Ibid.*, p. 94.

32. My point is certainly not that Bernard was the most important, or even first important, Christian thinker to address war in the context of Christian ethics. He was neither. Historically, his contribution does not lay in having made the ends and means of war morally acceptable in the last resort; SS Augustine and Thomas Aquinas, among other catholic teachers, have done this with greater theological precision than Bernard. Nor should we overemphasize Bernard's understanding of war and crusade as occasions for moral improvement; his general purpose for expressing himself on these matters was to maintain the hegemony of Christendom in the Holy Land.

   St Bernard's original contribution to the Christianization of war, I believe, was his insistence that states and individuals have an obligation in justice and charity to get on with the fighting once the last resort has been reached. And although Bernard applied this teaching to specifically religious wars, it also seems to me to have some relevance to wars fought for secular reasons, by Christians and others, when principles of justice and charity are at stake.

   Many today dismiss the rationale of 'holy war' as a mistaken and outdated form of religious enthusiasm, a manifestation of barbarity and violence that is difficult, if not impossible, to reconcile with Christ's teachings. The theological historian Bernard McGinn, for example, finds it possible to characterize as 'perverse' the development, which began in the mature thought of Augustine some seven hundred years before Bernard took up the subject (*The Crusades* [General Learning Press, 1973] p. 3). McGinn, Jean Leclercq, and other scholars rightly call attention to Bernard's far greater position in history as a man of peace than as a man of war. But we must admit that he was a man of war, and war of a very intransigent sort.

   Before uncritically accepting the negative judgments and implications about Bernard's advocacy of armed combat under certain conditions, and edging away from whatever general

lessons may still be discoverable in that advocacy, we should
examine the foundation of the criticism. Perhaps it is founded
on a pacifism that renounces all use of force. This is the
attitude Bernard himself taught as the only one appropriate for
clerics, although he obviously considered its absolute application foreign to authentic Christian tradition.

But the anti-holy war criticism may also be founded on a
modern religious indifferentism which forbids itself from taking any political action in the name of 'truth.' Then the
specific assertion (that the ends and means of war are funda-
mentally incompatible with Christ's message, selectively understood) may in reality derive from the broader principle that
religion and public policy ought to have nothing to do with
each other.

We no longer live in twelfth-century Europe, and it may
be that Bernard's formulation of Christianized, holy war is
not entitled to serve as an example to us today. But for
great numbers of people the formulation will not be discredit-
ed by arguments based on absolute pacifism or religious indifferentism. See Bernard Flood, 'St Bernard's View of Crusade'
(*Cistercian Studies*, 9:1, 1974); John Cleland, 'Foundations
of Crusade Theology' (*Faith and Reason*, 1:2 and 3, 1975); and
Jean Leclercq, 'Saint Bernard's Attitude.'

33. Georges Cattaui, *St Bernard of Clairvaux*, tr. E. Dargan (Dublin,
1966) p. 99. Cattaui here cites Davy, who, in *Saint Bernard*,
'has said with truth that the special achievement of Citeaux is
to have attained (in the terminology of the *Quest for the Grail*)
a glimpse of the secrets, the hidden glories, the mysteries of
God. For Citeaux is, unquestionably, the greatest of those who
profess the doctrine of love as the path to ecstasy.'

THE ENTRANCE OF THE CISTERCIANS
INTO THE CHURCH HIERARCHY 1098-1227:
THE BERNARDINE INFLUENCE

Joel Lipkin

Perhaps the most perplexing aspect of Bernard of Clairvaux's
mentality was his ability to combine, without any apparent tension,
an intense spirituality and a practical grasp of political reality.
The modern observer's difficulties in trying to reconcile these un-
avoidably colors his attempts to explain the saint's political activity. Scholars have generally approached the problem by interpret-
ing writings (such as the *De consideratione*) that relate to Church
government or by investigating the part Bernard played in the Anacletian schism or in disputed episcopal elections.[1] Their conclusions have covered the full spectrum of possibility from the sug-
gestion that Bernard rejected the high gregorian edifice *in toto*
to the notion that during the period 1130-1153 he, in effect, controlled the Papacy.

This paper proposes to approach Bernard's attitudes by investigating a somewhat neglected segment of the Cistercian Order: those
monks who, by their election as bishops and archbishops, by elevation to the Cardinalate, and by employment as papal legates, became integral members of the ecclesiastical hierarchy. Analyzing
Bernard's role in their appointment will, it is hoped, shed some
light on the political influence he exercised and, by extension,
his attitude towards the increasing centralization and institution-
alization of the Church.

My approach has been basically prosopographical; an attempt has
been made to gather relevant biographical information regarding
each cistercian bishop, archbishop, cardinal, and legate appointed
from the founding of the Order in 1098 to the death of Honorius III
in 1227. This time span seems sufficient to allow us to assess the
period of Bernard's influence in relation to that preceeding the
foundation of Clairvaux in 1115 and that following his death in 1153.
For each dignitary information regarding upbringing (family, social
status, and education), affiliation, position within the Order, and
positions held within the Church hierarchy has been sought. Relevant chronology, when available, is included.

The materials needed for such an investigation have been readily
available for many years. The *Päpste, Kardinäle und Bishöfe aus
dem Cistercienser-Orden* of Dominicus Willi (himself a cistercian
bishop) is a highly reliable guide.[2] As the size of the College of
Cardinals fluctuated significantly during this period, the number
of cistercian Cardinals appearing in Willi were compared with figures

for the total size of the cardinalate found in Johannes Brixius'
Die Mitglieder des Kardinalkollegiums and Conrad Eubel's *Hierarchia Catholica Medii Aevi.*[3] A series of interlocking german
dissertations have provided a nearly complete picture of legatine
activity in France, Germany, and Italy, along with occasional
glimpses into England, Scandinavia, and the East.[4] While absolute
completeness and accuracy regarding basic biographical data for
each cistercian dignitary elevated between 1098 to 1227 must remain an unattainable goal, and primary sources at times prove
contradictory, the prosopographical method will, if judiciously
utilized, provide general conclusions regarding the group as a
whole.

In the period under discussion, 1098–1227, nineteen cistercian
cardinals and one hundred fifty-one bishops and archbishops were
identified. Of the latter, twenty entered the Order only after
resigning their sees. These twenty will be excluded from the following discussion as the Order obviously played no role in their
formation or appointment. Such resignations testify to the spiritual and moral prestige of the Order but are not relevant to a study
of its political role.

As one might expect for this period, information regarding
monks' lives before they entered the Order is available for only
a minority of the cistercian dignitaries. The tendency for information regarding the aristocracy to survive in greater abundance
than that for other classes and the incompleteness of the data as
a whole makes confident generalization impossible. Given this, and
what is known about the background of members of the church hierarchy in general, it is probably not surprising that, without exception, those dignitaries about whom information is available were
all from aristocratic families; several were themselves related to
other bishops and cardinals; a few had been cathedral canons or
officers before entering the Order; some (like Otto of Freising)
were members of the highest ranks of society. Information about
their education is even less complete than biographical detail,
and only a few appear to have attended one of the newly emerging
universities.[5]

It is also important to distinguish the men who provided the
Order's political leadership from those who were its spiritual
leaders. While six of our subjects were canonized and five others
given the title 'blessed,' these men did not on the whole contribute to the formation of cistercian spirituality. Charles de Visch,
Bibliotheca scriptorum sacri Ordinis Cisterciensis, Johannes Schneyer, *Repertorium der lateinischen Sermones des Mittelalters,* and Eugene Manning, *Dictionnaire des auteurs cisterciens,* indicate literary
works by less than thirty of these dignitaries.[6] Scanning a list
of cistercian bishops, archbishops, and cardinals, one finds several
of major political importance within the Church, but one is more apt

to be surprised that these men were Cistercians than to find they
were of importance in the intellectual development of the Order.[7]

   With this sketchy introduction as background let us turn to
the application of basic quantitative techniques to these one hundred fifty Cistercians. There emerge several significant conclusions regarding the make-up of this seemingly uncharacteristic
cistercian elite as well as an indication of the role Bernard himself played in their appointment. As the number of appointments
in any given year is small and subject to fluctuation, the graphs
used to illustrate these results are based on cumulative statistics
rather than new appointments. That is, for any given year they represent the total number of Cistercians then in office rather than
the number newly appointed.[8]

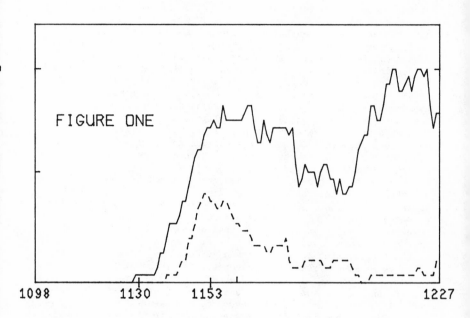

FIGURE ONE

1098   1130   1153   1227

Figure One represents the results of this analysis applied to
the episcopate. The x-axis covers the time period 1098 to 1227.
Marks indicate dates that have emerged during analysis as crucial:
1130, the beginning of the schism, and 1153, the year of Bernard's
death. The y-axis indicates the number of Cistercians in office.
The solid-line graph in Figure One represents the total number of
cistercian bishops and archbishops in office during each year. The
broken-line graph is limited to those who, prior to their appointment, had been monks of Clairvaux.

While statistical analysis is generally insufficient to demonstrate causal relationships, certain aspects of these graphs do
seem suggestive. The first election of a Cistercian (Peter of Tar-
antaise) occurred at the beginning of the Anacletian schism. While
he was abbot of La Ferté, for the next quarter century monks from
a single house, Clairvaux, dominated the episcopal activity of the
Order, although several of these men left Clairvaux and became abbots at other Cistercian houses prior to their election. Thus Clairvaux may be seen as a 'training center' for an elite group of Cistercians who, as abbots, became the leaders of the Order and, as high
ecclesiastics, leaders of the Church. In the 1130's, constituting

more than three-quarters of the Cistercian bishops and archbishops
in office, men who had been monks at Bernard's house never held
significantly less than half the total number of cistercian sees
until after the Saint's death. Following it, Clairvaux's proportion declined precipitantly. From having twelve bishops in 1152-
1153, Clairvaux declined in importance until at any time from 1180
to the end of this study there were never more than three contemporary bishops who had been monks in that house. Total cistercian
appointments similarly declined following Bernard's death (largely
because of a decline in numbers at Clairvaux) but where the Cistercian appointments recovered to pre-1153 levels, Clairvaux's candi-
dates continued in decline. This was due not to a shift in focus
to another house but rather to a diffusion of appointments throughout the Order as a whole.

The correlation between the geographical location of the houses
and the offices held by cistercian dignitaries is represented in
Tables One and Two.[9] Table One represents the distribution prior
to Bernard's death; Table Two the situation following 1153. Monks
were frequently resident in more than one house before entering the
hierarchy and once invested might be translated. This is reflected
in the tables; that is, a single individual may be counted several
times as he moved from house to house and was translated from one
diocese to another. Those few dioceses that had more than one
cistercian bishop or archbishop are indicated separately. The nu-
meral in parentheses following each see represents the total number of Cistercians to hold that see and thus counteracts the ten-
dancy of the table to overstate apparent cistercian representation.
Dioceses that had only one cistercian prelate are grouped together
within the appropriate geographical unit. Suffragan sees are treated as a separate category.

HOUSES

	France	Germany	Italy	Ireland	England & Scotland	Unknown	Total
CARDINALS (7)	6	0	1	0	0	1	8
BISHOPRICS:							
FRANCE and NETHERLANDS	18	4	0	0	0	0	22
Tarantaise (2)	(3)						
Reims (2)	(2)						
GERMANY	2	4	0	0	0	0	6
ITALY	6	0	2	0	0	2	10
IRELAND	0	0	0	2	0	1	3
ENGLAND	2	0	0	0	1	0	3
TOTAL	34	8	3	2	1	4	52

Table One

HOUSES

	France & Netherlands	Germany	Italy	Ireland	England & Scotland	Spain	Scandinavia	Eastern Europe	Unknown	Total
CARDINALS (12)	13	1	1	0	0	0	0	0	1	16
BISHOPRICS: FRANCE and NETHERLANDS	38	2	1	0	1	7	0	0	0	49
Arras (2)	(3)									
Bourges (3)	(6)									
Perpignan (3)						(3)				
Rennes (2)	(3)									
GERMANY	0	4	0	0	0	0	0	0	0	4
ITALY	5	0	13	0	0	0	0	0	6	24
Sassari (2)									(1)	
Sora (3)										
IRELAND	0	0	0	12	1	0	0	0	6	19
Cashel (2)				(1)						
Clogers (2)				(2)						
Leighlin (2)				(2)						
ENGLAND and SCOTLAND	0	0	0	0	12	0	0	0	1	13
Man (3)					(3)				(1)	
SPAIN	1	0	0	0	0	5	0	0	2	9
Osma (2)	(1)					(1)			(1)	
SCANDINAVIA	1	0	0	0	0	0	4	0	2	7
Upsala (2)							(2)			
EASTERN EUROPE	0	3	0	0	0	0	0	3	0	6
SUFFRAGANS	5	1	0	0	0	1	0	0	1	8
TOTALS	63	11	16	12	14	13	4	3	19	155

Table Two

Localizing tendencies are evident in both tables; cistercian bishops tended to have been monks in houses located in the general region of their sees. The regional breakdown based on modern geographical boundaries utilized here is not a fully satisfactory means of demonstrating this relationship. General tendencies towards localization nevertheless seem clear. Indeed, there are several cases of a Cistercian being elevated to the see of the diocese in which his house was located.

The tables also illustrate a change in the pattern of the elevation of cistercian dignitaries following Bernard's death. In thirty-four of the fifty-two events (65%) recorded in Table One the house of origin was within the borders of modern France: in Table Two the proportion declines to sixty-three of one hundred fifty-five (41%). Interestingly, the proportion of cistercian appointments to french bishoprics, when compared to total cistercian appointments, does not undergo as marked a decline (42% to 32%) after 1153. This indicates that french monasteries declined as 'training centers' for cistercian bishops and archbishops in other countries. While french cathedrals continued to elect a greater proportion of cistercian dignitaries than did other regions, here again a leveling similar to that seen within the order was evidenced.

One must stress that Cistercians never dominated the european episcopate. Their total number was always small, never exceeding twenty-nine men in office at any given time. Only in Ireland did they constitute an appreciable proportion of a nation's episcopate between 1098-1227. No diocese had more than three Cistercians as bishops during that period. But within the Order, Clairvaux clearly predominated as a source of cistercian bishops and archbishops during Bernard's tenure as abbot.

Turning to the cardinalate, one may advance similar conclusions. Again 1130 saw the first Cistercian, Martin Cibo, elevated to the College of Cardinals. Of the nineteen cistercian cardinals, seven had been monks at Clairvaux. But if one divides these figures around the crucial year 1153, Clairvaux's role becomes even clearer. Of the seven Cistercians who became cardinals in the twenty-six years prior to that date, five had been monks under Bernard. In the following seven decades only two of twelve cistercian cardinals came from Clairvaux. As was the case for the episcopacy, cistercian cardinals never dominated the College. No more than three Cistercians were elevated during any single pontificate (the highest proportion being Eugenius III's three Cistercians out of nineteen appointments).

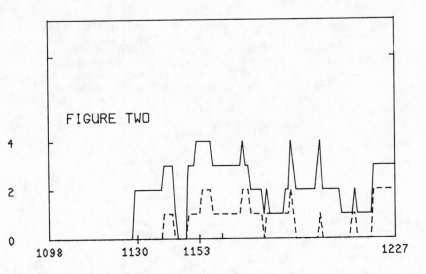

FIGURE TWO

The solid line graph in Figure Two represents the total number of cistercian cardinals in office year by year, and as can be readily seen their numbers were always small. Analysis of their titular churches, however, produces an interesting result. Of the nineteen cistercian cardinals, ten were cardinal bishops. Although even here they never constituted a majority, (as can be seen from the broken line) the concentration of Cistercians in the seven suburbicarian sees is some indication of the prestige accorded them, and is of particular interest when set in the context of the point at issue in the disputed election of 1130. While Cistercians never constituted the *maior pars* of the College, they formed a significant portion of what supporters of Innocent II had in 1130 designated as the *sanior pars*.

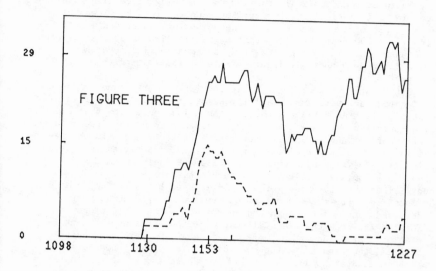

FIGURE THREE

Figure Three represents the summation of Figure One and the related data for the cardinalate. As one can readily see, the addition of this new data does not alter the overall movements and shapes of the graphs represented in Figure One.

Turning finally to Cistercian legates, one finds that the raw data is even less clear-cut than information on the cardinalate and the episcopacy. Not only is the coverage of legatine activity incomplete and the composition of the legations often uncertain, but during this period in which the precise legal definition of legate was being developed, one is often unsure whether a man identified as a Cistercian is a legate *a latere,* a judge delegate, a papal nuncio, or a standing legate. Even though all except the last would indicate active cistercian involvement in papal government, and standing legates have wherever possible been eliminated from the totals, it must be stressed that these results necessarily remain provisional. Casting them into mathematical terms ought not to conceal the uncertainties that underlie them. At best they may be interpreted as indicators of the changing cistercian involvement in ecclesiatical government; they ought not to be viewed as accurate or absolute measures of the number of cistercian legates. Finally, it ought to be clear that a quantitative study that attempts to measure the importance of a group by counting its legates must necessarily assume that all legations are of equal importance, a dubious proposition at best.

With that caveat, I offer these results. There is no evidence of legatine activity among Cistercians prior to 1130. Under Innocent II, Bernard fulfilled several commissions but, with that exception, only two of the sixty-nine appointments identified prior to the pontificate of Anastasius IV were made to Cistercians. In the remaining years of the twelfth century cistercian activity increased only slightly, although in the years 1159-69 twelve of Alexander III's eighty-six commissions went to Cistercians. It was only under Innocent III that Cistercians were regularly used by the Papacy. Of his one hundred fifty-three commissions, twenty went to members of the Order. His successor maintained approximately the same proportion of Cistercian legates. Thus, if one were to represent the contribution of Cistercians to overall legatine activity in the period 1083-1227, the resultant graph would be quite unlike those drawn to represent bishops and cardinals. It would remain at zero until 1130, hover near that mark until the 1150's, fluctuate at a somewhat higher level for the remainder of the century, and rise to encompass perhaps one-eighth of the total legatine appointments for the first three decades of the thirteenth century. Relating the data for legates to the more comprehensive and accurate material available for cardinals, archbishops, and bishops has proved to be a difficult task. The 1150's again seem to be a turning point, but in this case quantity increases rather than decreases. Perhaps Bernard's influence was again at work, here in his ability to check the involvement of monks in the highly active role necessarily played by papal legates.

In an analysis of the results of this study as a whole, however, two points are clear. First, the Anacletian schism must be seen as a major turning point in cistercian history, for it was then that members of the Order first became members of the ecclesiastical hierarchy. Second, Bernard's role in this innovation seems clearly demonstrated both by the central role played by Clairvaux during his abbacy and by the changes in the volume and nature of cistercian ecclesiastical appointments that followed his death.

I hope that this paper has usefully surveyed the ecclesiastical activities of a somewhat obscure and unusual group of early Cistercians and by doing so has illuminated a previously unstudied aspect of Bernard of Clairvaux's role within the Order and in relationship to the high gregorian Church. Methodologically, it may demonstrate that the application of quantitative techniques to prosopographical data previously of only antiquarian interest can shed light on areas of history not usually thought to be amenable to this sort of analysis.

When in the seventeenth century Gaspar Jongelinus entitled his rather unreliable list of cistercian members of the Church hierarchy *Purpura divi Bernardi* he was more correct than he could possibly have realized.

The Catholic University of America and
The Planning Research Corporation, McLean.

NOTES

1. E.g. Bernard Jacqueline, *Papauté et épiscopat selon Saint Bernard de Clairvaux* (Saint-Lo, 1963), and Joseph R. Leahey, 'The Influence of St. Bernard on Episcopal Elections in France, 1138-1153--Reims, Bourges, Auxerre' (Ph.D. diss., Fordham University, 1973).

2. (Bregenz, 1912).

3. Brixius, (Berlin, 1912); Eubel, vol. 1 (Münster, 1913).

4. O. Frommel, *Die päpstliche Legationsgewalt in deutschen Reiche während des 10., 11.* Schumann, *Die päpstlichen Legaten in Deutschland zur Zeit Heinrichs IV. und Heinrichs V., 1056-1125* (diss., Marburg, 1912): J. Bachmann, *Die päpstlichen Legaten in Deutschland und Skandinavien, 1125-1159* in *Historische Studien 115.* O. Englemann, *Die päpstlichen Legaten in Deutschland bis zur Mitte des II. Jahrhunderts* (diss., Marburg, 1913). H. Zimmermann, *Die päpstliche Legation in der ersten Hälfte des 13. Jahrhunderts, vom Regierungsantritt Innocenz' III. bis zum Tode Gregors IX., 1198-1241* (Paderborn, 1913). H. Tillmann, *Die päpstlichen Legaten in England bis zur Beendigung der Legation Gualas, 1218* (diss., Bonn, 1926). W. Ohnsorge, *Die Legaten Alexanders III. im ersten Jahrzehnt seines Pontifikats, 1159-1169 in historische studien 175.* I. Friedlaender, *Die päpstlichen Legaten in Deutschland und Italien am Ende des XII. Jahrhunderts, 1181-1198 in Historische Studien 177.* T. Schieffer, *Die päpstlichen Legaten in Frankreich vom Vertrage von Meersen (870) bis zum Schisma von 1130, Historische Studien* 263. W. Janssen, *Die päpstlichen Legaten in Frankreich vom Schisma Anaclets II. bis zum Tode Coelistins III., 1130-1198* (Cologne, 1961).

5. In most cases the university-educated bishops listed in Willi only became Cistercians after resigning their sees. The corporate entrance of the Cistercians into the universities post-dates the period under discussion. Stephen of Lexington founded the first Cistercian *studium*, the College du Chardonnet, at Paris in 1246 for monks of Clairvaux. It was later opened to monks of the Order as a whole.

6. de Visch (Köln, 1655); Schneyer, four volumes in progress, 'Beiträge zur Geschichte der Philosophie und Theologie des Mittelalters, Neue Folge, 43:1-4 (Münster im W., 1969-72); Manning, six fascicules in the *Documentation Cistercienne* 16 (Rochefort, 1975-9).

7. Baldwin of Ford, Bishop of Worchester and later Archbishop of Canterbury, ought to be noted as an exception to this generalization.

8. Statistically the two are closely related, but the cumulative analysis tends to smooth out non-significant yearly variation and thus provide the basis for a more coherent graphical representation.

9. Sources: P. Leopold Janauschek, *Originum Cisterciensium* (Vienna, 1877), Frederic Van Der Meer, *Atlas de l'Ordre Cistercien* (Brussels, 1965), and Johann Graesse et al., *Orbis Latinus* 3 vols. (Braunschweig, 1972).

ST BERNARD AND THE CISTERCIAN OFFICE
AT THE ABBEY OF THE PARACLETE

CHRYSOGONUS WADDELL, O.C.S.O.

The historian interested in the stormy relationship between Peter Abelard and Bernard of Clairvaux need complain of no dearth of pertinent source material. But what of the contacts between Heloise and Bernard? On the basis of the documentation heretofore exploited by scholars, even the most imaginative historian would be hard put to find enough material for more than a modest footnote. Indeed, only once does Bernard's name enter directly into the history of the Paraclete, or, possibly--if we are willing to stretch the evidence a bit--twice. In January of 1131, both Bernard and Peter were in the company of Pope Innocent II at the Abbey of Morigny, near Etampes.[1] No one can prove that, on this occasion, Bernard did *not* put in a good word for the community at the Paraclete, which became the glad recipient, towards the end of November of the same year, of the papal privilege *Quoties illud*.[2] We are on much firmer ground as regards the one and only documented visit paid by Bernard to Heloise and her nuns, probably after 1131, but before Peter's friendly rapport with Bernard degenerated into bitter enmity.[3] For it is from Peter himself that we learn about this visit, in his *Letter 10*--the only extant letter addressed by him to Bernard;[4] and, as of the writing of this letter, Peter and Bernard seem to have been on the best of terms. We might understandably discount the 'venerable' and 'most dear' of the salutation as no more than an epistolary convention, but it would be difficult to discount, in the same manner, Peter's reference to Bernard's special love for him--*ea caritate, qua me praecipue amplectimini*-- and to his own desire of avoiding even the slightest offence against the abbot of Clairvaux.[5] And surely Peter was sincere in this protestation of friendship. Years later, not long before the fateful council convoked at Sens in 1140, Peter was to write a group of disciples that, till then, Bernard had always pretended to be not only a friend, but a most dear friend--*amicum, immo amicissimum*.[6]

As Peter tells it, Heloise and her community had been looking forward to Bernard's visit for a long time, but it was a visit well worth waiting for. Bernard's eloquence on the occasion had been more that of an angel than of a mere mortal; and, when Heloise later gave Peter her impressions, these were still so vivid that she spoke only with the greatest exultation--*summa exsultatione*.[7]

It is curious that it was a point of liturgical usage which occasioned Peter's description of this visit of Bernard to Heloise. Bernard had been a bit surprised to hear, in the Lord's Prayer as prayed at the Paraclete, the words 'supersubstantial bread' rather than the standard 'daily bread.' Peter's somewhat defensive reaction was to write an *apologia* for this apparent innovation and to draw up a long catalogue of Cistercian liturgical oddities and innovations.[8] According to Peter, it was a case of the pot calling the kettle black.

Hell hath no fury like a woman scorned--unless, perhaps, it is the deeply passionate, loyal woman who has to look on while the man she loves is forced to bite the dust in humiliation and unconditional surrender. One need be no great expert in feminine psychology to surmise that, as the friendship between Peter and Bernard quickly turned to hostility, Heloise's attitude towards Bernard underwent a dramatic and precipitous change. But let us not be too hasty in our recourse to popular psychology. The truth of the matter is that, whatever might have been Heloise's personal opinion of Bernard in the aftermath of Peter's bitter defeat, she nevertheless was responsible for reforming the Paraclete Divine Office along Cistercian lines. Further, the Cistercian liturgical books she drew upon were the books reformed under Bernard's personal aegis, sometime around 1147.

BERNARD AND THE CISTERCIAN LITURGY

The year 1147 is something of a watershed in the history of the liturgy of the White Monks; for this was the year--or the approximate year--which marked the end of an important program of liturgical reform. This reform was so dramatically successful that, for many centuries, it was thought that no Cistercian liturgical relics of the pre-1147 period managed to survive.[9]

One of the few contemporary documents to refer to this liturgical reform is the 'long form' of the *Life of Saint Stephen of Obazine*.[10] In 1142, Stephen turned his community of hermits into a community of cenobites. Though not officially affiliated with the Cistercian Order, the monks of Obazine nevertheless did their best to follow the Cistercian way of life, even as regards liturgical books and points of ritual. In 1147, Obazine and its dependent communities were incorporated into the Cistercian Order--but not without irritating consequences for the scribes of the Obazine scriptorium. Stephen's biographer--who was a monk of Obazine at the time--tells us that some of the liturgical books so painfully transcribed in or after 1142 had to be abandoned and then replaced by totally new versions, while other books could be retained only with a certain amount of erasures and over-writing.[11] Why the need of all this scribal activity? Simply because of the fact that, sometime before 1147, a reform of the Cistercian liturgical books had taken place at the level of the entire Order. Why the need for this reform? Well, 'you should realize that the books which the

Cistercians first used for the liturgy were completely shot through
with corruptions and mistakes.'[12] Our narrator here exaggerates a
bit. As we shall see, the book with the Office chants, the book
with the Mass chants, and the hymnbook were the real offenders, while
the several other books required for the celebration of the liturgy
were in need of only occasional re-touches in order to pass muster.
At any rate, the defective books remained in use 'till the time of
Saint Bernard. In his time, by common decree of the abbots [of the
General Chapter], the books were corrected and emended by the same
holy abbot and his cantors, in the version such as is had at present.'[13]

The anonymous biographer's account is vouched for by Bernard
himself, who, in his own Prologue to the Cistercian Antiphonary--
the book with Office chants--confirms the fact that the General
Chapter had appointed him to supervise the revision of the antiphonary.[14] This important work of revision of texts and melodies,
however, was no one-man job. Bernard writes that he summoned to
Clairvaux, for this purpose, an unspecified number of abbots skill-
ed in the theory and practice of music.[15] One of these was almost
certainly Guy, abbot of Cherlieu, and probable author of a chant
treatise which supplied ideas operative in the reform of the melodies.[16] Another member of the group was surely Richard, who was
re-called from Vauclair, where he had been abbot, became cantor at
Clairvaux, and was subsequently sent to his native England as abbot
of Fountains at a critical moment in its history.

THE LITURGICAL BOOKS OF THE PARACLETE

For our present purposes, two, and only two manuscripts in-
vite our attention. Both are relatively late; and this circum-
stance might explain their having been neglected by scholars--
though not entirely neglected.

The first and earliest manuscript represents a relative late-
comer to the liturgical scene. It is a *liber ordinarius* or ordinal, and I shall refer to it as the Paraclete Ordinal (PO).[17] Even
in the late thirteenth century, when this manuscript was written,
the various books needed for the celebration of the liturgy formed
a small library. The purpose of the ordinal[18] was to give clear
directions how all the various texts and chants scattered throughout many different books were to be coordinated, so that the liturgical celebrations could be carried out without too many disasterous occurences. But there was no set norm concerning how such a
book was to be organized, or what exactly it should contain. Thus,
many ordinals are rather akin to monastic customaries, and PO contains not only rubrics about the liturgy proper, but also about
what is to be read in refectory and before Compline, and what day

the annual hair cutting is to be done. The scatterbrained nun who was the scrivener of PO was no great credit to the memory of Heloise. Her script is clear, firm, even attractive, but she was not quite able to cope with the challenge presented by the redaction of this manuscript. First of all, she was clearly working from a Latin model of sorts, attempting to render it into Old French, without bothering first to shape up a quick first draft, and her Latin was much better than her French. Secondly, she was working almost certainly from a much corrected manuscript from an earlier age--one with many erasures, marginal additions and clarifications, and scraps of inserted material written in a dozen different hands. Only in this way can we explain the occasional reversal of the proper order of things, or the reduplication of more or less the same directives for the same particular rite. There are instances of synodal decrees requiring priests to consult their *liber ordinarius* for details concerning the next day's Office, with a view to avoiding mishaps.[19] In the case of PO, observance of such a directive would have spelled disaster. Still, the manuscript yields treasures on every page, and is considerably more exciting to work with than the precise, detailed, and logically arranged ordinals penned by scribes of a more professional caliber. Actually, our manuscript is a composite one, consisting of three distinct books. The first is a 'book of burials,' giving *obits* of nuns and other persons connected with the Paraclete, and indicating their precise place of burial.[20] The same wide variety of hands which kept this first book up to date till the sixteenth century have also been at work in the ordinal proper, which is the second book in the manuscript. Finally, there is a slightly lacunose processional, written almost entirely in Latin, and giving only the text-*incipits* for the chants used in this procession-prone abbey.

Our second manuscript dates probably from the very early fifteenth century.[21] Scholars who have taken note of it have invariably described it as a *diurnal*--that is to say, a breviary with only the Day Hours, from Lauds onwards. But this is clearly a serious mistake. It should be remembered that the modern type of breviary emerged only as a relatively late phenomenon. At an earlier age, elements from the many different books used for the celebration of the Office were tossed together under a single cover, but in ways which varied so much from manuscript to manuscript, that it becomes rather difficult at times to classify certain compilations--like the present one.[22] Our manuscript contains a complete hymnal repertory, with all the hymns required for Matins--the Night Office-- as well as for the Day Hours. This manuscript also incorporates all the elements of that little studied liturgical book called the collectar or *collectaneum*. This particular book contained all the Office collects and short readings or *capitula* recited by the hebdomadary, that is to say, the weekly official who, under the abbot

or abbess, presided at the Office; and, so often as Matins material
is required by the hebdomadary, it can be found in this compilation.
Finally, our manuscript contains the texts of all the chants--anti-
phons, responsories of various kinds, and versicles and responsories
--needed for the Day Hours, but also for Matins on ferial days
throughout the year, and during the more important liturgical seasons. There is also a complete calendar in which, as we shall see,
the Cistercian presence at the Paraclete looms large, and also a
goodly number of odds and ends which need to be studied carefully
to get a good grasp of the special character of the liturgy of this
abbey. Since our manuscript is very much more than a *diurnal*, but
very much less than a complete *breviary*, I shall refer to it simply as the Office Book (OBk).

In each of sections immediately following, I shall sketch in
the briefest possible terms something of the history of the Cistercian liturgical book which has been purloined by the nuns of the
Paraclete; after which I shall describe, with equal brevity, how
this material has been used incorporated, with or without adapta-
tions, into the Paraclete liturgy. Only afterwards will we be in
a position to draw tentative conclusions as to the date of the profound 'cistercianization' of the Paraclete Office, and as to the
motive or motives for such a change.

THE CISTERCIAN CALENDAR

The Cistercian calendar of the twelfth century is absolutely
sui generis, and can be explained only in terms of contingent historical factors and liturgical preoccupations virtually proper to
the White Monks of this period.

My own preoccupation in matters of twentieth-century Cistercian calendar reform put me into possession of the documentation
needed for a reasonably accurate genetic history of the evolution
of the early twelfth-century Cistercian calendar. From a study and
comparison of the many documents bearing on the subject, the following points emerge.

1. The Cistercian calendar has as its distant ancestor the
calendar of the great abbey of Montier-la-Celle, near Troyes. It
was there that Saint Robert, future abbot founder of Cîteaux, entered upon his life as a monk, and functioned as prior for many
years. His few years as ill-starred abbot of Saint-Michel de Ton-
nerre were only a minor interruption of his association with the
liturgical tradition of Montier-la-Celle, which was also to be
found at Saint-Ayoul, where Robert also spent a short time as superior prior to the foundation, first of Collan, then, in 1075,
of Molesme.[23] Collation of Molesme breviary material with the relatively abundant remains of the Montier-la-Celle breviary, shows

that the Molesme Office was virtually identical with that of Robert's
first monastery. As for the Molesme calendar, it is simply a drastic
simplification of the Montier-la-Celle calendar.[24]

2. The calendar of the earliest extant Cistercian breviary--
which can be dated 1132, or soon thereafter--is, in its turn, only
a simplification of the Molesme calendar.[25] This calendar, however,
has been modified with a view towards conformity with two normative
documents.

a. Because Saint Benedict, in Chapter 14 of his *Holy Rule*,
patterns the Office for solemnities and feasts of saints on the Sunday Office, with its twelve Night Office readings and responsories,
the Cistercians excluded the Three Lesson feasts standard everywhere.[26]
Since it was clearly impossible to assign all the saints in the calendar a Twelve Lesson Office, the less important celebrations were reduced to a simple commemoration at Lauds and Vespers, consisting of
an antiphon, versicle and response, and collect tacked on to the Office after the dismissal verse had been sung. In addition, most of
these commemorations called for a conventual Mass of the saint or
saints, but the number of such Masses was drastically reduced in the
reform of around 1147.

b. Also normative for the Cistercians was the sanctoral
cycle of the ancient sacramentary--the liturgical book with the Mass
prayers--which they had adopted at an early date. My own working hy-
pothesis is that the Cistercian version was based almost exclusively
on a sacramentary of the papal chapel, dating from the end of the
eleventh century, but still relatively faithful to a much older model, and with surprisingly few tenth-and eleventh-century additions
to the sober sanctoral cycle of an older period. All the extant Cistercian manuscripts of the pre-1147 period--and these include a breviary, two evangeliaries, an epistolary, and two sacramentaries[27]
--have the same curious arrangement: only the saints included in
the sanctoral cycle of the unidentified prototype manuscript have a
place in the main body of the book. All the other saints are rele-
gated to the Common, with almost no exception.

THE PARACLETE CALENDAR

Due to the somewhat chaotic arrangement of PO, our surest
source of knowledge about the Paraclete calendar is OBk, whose
calendar is preserved intact, ff. 2r-7v. Not that this calendar
is without mistakes! These can easily be controlled, however, by
checking the calendar entry against the corresponding material in
the body of the manuscript. Both PO and its processional supple-
ment supply further checks.

In brief, our Paraclete nuns have simply adopted the Cistercian calendar in the form it had around 1147. On the Cistercian

side, there were a few calendar changes spanning the years 1175 to
1180/1182;[28] so the absence of this later material indicates a reform of the Paraclete calendar sometime between 1147 and--more or
less--1175.

Our nuns, however, have managed to retain important material
from their earlier tradition. They have also rather often raised
a Cistercian commemoration to the rank of a Twelve Lesson feast.
The fidelity with which the original Cistercian calendar has been
preserved, however, has led to more than a slight amount of illogic
as regards the order of entries in the Paraclete calendar. The generally accepted practice has always been that, so often as there are
two celebrations of unequal rank on the same day, the higher ranking
celebration comes first. Now, days with two commemorations are rather frequent in the Cistercian calendar; and, from time to time, the
Paraclete nuns have raised the second entry to the rank of a Twelve
Lesson feast, but without disturbing the original order. So also
in the several instances in which a feast proper to the Paraclete
is celebrated on a day already occupied by a commemoration from
the Cistercian calendar: the commemoration entry retains its original position, while the higher ranking feast is added in the second place.

Since the topic under discussion is not so much the Paraclete
liturgy as it is the Cistercian contribution to the Paraclete liturgy, this is not the place to discuss the extremely interesting features proper to the Paraclete entries. In general, it can be noted
that commemorations and feasts of women saints are given pride of
place, that a number of sanctoral entries are explicable chiefly
in terms of Abelard's personal history and influence,[29] and that
there seems to have been a special devotion to the seven 'deacons'
of the *Acts of the Apostles*, whom Abelard frequently extolled as
models for clerics assigned to the pastoral care of women. In view
of the relatively late date of the manuscript of OBk, one is a bit
puzzled by the relatively few signs of evolution in the calendar.
There are obvious reasons why Bernard--canonized in 1174--does not
appear in the sanctoral. But what did the Paraclete nuns have a-
gainst Dominic and Francis of Assisi?

The following Table makes clear the relationship between the
Paraclete calendar and its Cistercian model. In the left hand column are given the entries common to both calendars; in the right
hand column are the entries proper to the Paraclete calendar. Twelve
Lesson feasts are indicated by capital letters, commemorations by
lower case letters. An asterisk next to a Cistercian commemoration
--com*--indicates that, in the Paraclete calendar, this commemoration is raised to Twelve Lesson rank. Omitted among the Paraclete
entries are, of course, the several very late additions which have
nothing corresponding to them in PO or in the body of OBk. Also
omitted are a few Paraclete entries *Vigilia. Missa*, which refe-

the vigil of certain feasts: there is a vigil Mass, but the Office
is in no way affected. So often as this entry *does* affect the Office,
it has been retained. In a number of instances, the Paraclete scribe
has added the term *missa* to *commemoratio,* thus indicating not only an
Office commemoration, but a proper conventual Mass; however, this addition has been made so inconsistently that, for the purposes of com-
paring our two calendars, such additions have been ignored.

CITEAUX AND PARACLETE   PARACLETE ONLY

I A N U A R I U S

1 CIRCUMCISIO DOMINI XII

2 Octavae S. Stephani com*

3 Octavae S. Iohannis com*

4 Octavae SS. Innocentium com*

5   Vigilia. Missa.[30]

6 EPIPHANIA DOMINI XII

10 Pauli primi heremitae com   Nichanoris conf. unus de

                                      septem com

13 OCTAVAE EPIPHANIAE XII

   Hilarii et Remigii epp com[31]

14 Felicis in Pincis com

15 Mauri abbatis com   Boniti ep et conf [com]

16 Marcelli papae et mart com

17 Speusippi, Eleusippi et Meleusippi

     martyrum com   Antonii atque Sulpitii
                                    conf [XII][32]

18 Priscae virg et mart com

20 FABIANI ET SEBASTIANI martyrum XII

21 AGNETIS virg et mart XII

22 VINCENTII mart   XII

23 Emerentianae virg et mart   com*

25 CONVERSIO S. PAULI   XII

   Praeiecti   ep et mart   com

28 Agnetis secundo   com*

29

                                        GILDAE abbatis XII

                              Papiae et Mauri martyrum   com

30

                                   Aldegundis   virg   com

                    F E B R U A R I U S

1 Ignatii   ep et mart   com

   Brigidae   virg   com

2 PURIFICATIO S. MARIAE   XII

3

                              BLASII ep et mart XII

5 AGATHAE virg et mart XII

6 Vedasti et Amandi   epp   com

10 Sotheris virg et mart   com

   Scholasticae virg   com*

14 Valentini   mart   com

   Vitalis, Feliculae, et Zenonis mart   com

16 Iulianae   virg et mart   com

22 CATHEDRA S. PETRI   XII

24 MATHIAE ap   XII

M A R T I U S

1 Albini ep com

12 GREGORII papae XII

21 BENEDICTI abbatis XII

25 ANNUNTIATIO DOMINICA XII

A P R I L I S

4 AMBROSII ep XII

9
                                    Prochori mart qui fuit unus

                                        de septem com

14 Tiburtii, Valeriani et Maximi mart com

19
                                    Timonis mart [unus de septum]

                                        com

23 Georgii mart com

25 MARCI ev XII

28 Vitalis mart com

M A I U S

1 PHILIPPI ET IACOBI app XII

3 INVENTIO SANCTAE CRUCIS XII

   Alexandri, Eventii et Theodoli mart com

6 Iohannis apostoli ad portam latinam com*

10 Gordiani et Epimachi martyrum com

11   Mammerti ep com

12   Nerei, Achillei atque Pancratii mart com

19   Potentianae virg com

23   Desiderii ep et mart com

24   Donatiani et Rogatiani martyrum com

25   Urbani papae et mart com

31   Petronillae virg com

I U N I U S

1   Nichomedis mart com

2   Marcellini et Petri martyrum com

6   PHILIPPI qui fuit unus de

                            septem XII

8   Medardi ep com

9   Primi et Feliciani martyrum com

11   Barnabae ap com*

12   Basilidis, Cyrini, Naboris et Nazarii

      martyrum com

15   Viti mart com

16   Cirici et Iulitae martyrum com*

18   Marci et Marcelliani martyrum com

19   Gervasii et Prothasii martyrum com*

22   Albani mart com   ACHATII SOCIORUMQUE EIUS XII

23 Vigilia S. Iohannis Baptistae

24 NATIVITAS S. IOHANNIS BAPTISTAE   XII

25   Eligii ep et conf   com

26 Iohannis et Pauli martyrum   com

28 Vigilia Apostolorum

    Leonis papae   com

    Hyrenaei cum sociis suis   com

29 NATALE APOSTOLORUM PETRI ET PAULI   XII

30 COMMEMORATIO S. PAULI   XII   Albini ep et conf   com

I U L I U S

                                                      33

1   OCTAVAE S. IOHANNIS BAPTISTAE   XII   THEOBALDI conf XII

2   Processi et Martiniani   martyrum   com

4   Translatio S. Martini   com*

6   OCTAVAE APOSTOLORUM XII

10 Septem Fratrum   martyrum   com

11   TRANSLATIO S. BENEDICTI XII

17   ALEXII conf   XII

20   MARGARETAE virg et mart XII

21 Praxedis virg   com

22 MARIAE MAGDALENAE   XII

23 Apollinaris ep et mart   com

24 Christinae virg et mart   com

25 IACOBI ap XII

Christophori et Cucufati martyrum com

28 Nazarii, Celsi et Pantaleonis mart com

29 Felicis, ep et mart com

Simplicii, Faustini et Beatricis mart com

30 Abdon et Sennes martyrum com*

31 Germani ep com

A U G U S T U S

1 AD VINCULA S. PETRI XII

Machabaeorum com

Eusebii ep et mart com[34]

2 Stephani papae et mart com*

3 INVENTIO S. STEPHANI protomartyris XII

Gamalielis, Nichodemi atque
Abibon [com]

6 Sixti papae et mart com

TRANSFIGURATIO DOMINI XII

Felicissimi et Agapiti martyrum com Iusti et Pastoris [com][35]

7 Donati ep et mart com

8 Cyriaci cum sociis suis com[36]

9 Vigilia S. Laurentii

Romani mart Com replaced by: Secundiani et Romani com

10 LAURENTII mart XII

11 Tiburtii mart com

13 Hippolyti cum sociis suis com*   Radegundis Reginae com

14 Vigilia Sanctae Mariae

   Eusebii conf com

15 ASSUMPTIO SANCTAE MARIAE XII

17 Octavae S. Laurentii com*

   Mammeti mart com

18 Agapiti mart com

19 Magni mart com

22 OCTAVE SANCTAE MARIAE XII

   Timothei et Symphoriani [mart] com

23   QUIRIACERIS mart XII
                          37
24 BARTHOLOMEI ap XII

25 Genesii mart com   Eusebii, Pontiani, Vincentii

                                        et Peregrini mart com

27 Rufi mart com

28 AUGUSTINI ep ,XII

   Hermetis mart com

29 DECOLLATIO S. IOHANNIS BAPTISTAE XII

   Sabinae virg et mart com

30 Felicis et Adaucti martyrum com FIACRII conf XII

S E P T E M B E R

1   Egidii abbatis   com   <u>Replaced by</u>:   EGIDII abbatis [et]

    Prisci mart   com   LUPI ep XII [38]

3   AYGULPHI mart   XII

4   Marcelli   mart   com

7   Evurtii ep   com

8   NATIVITAS SANCTAE MARIAE   XII

    Adriani mart   com [39]

9   Gorgonii mart   com

11 Proti et Iacincti martyrum   com

14 EXALTATIO SANCTAE CRUCIS   XII

    Cornelii et Cypriani martyrum   com

15 Nichomedis mart   com

16 Eufemiae virg et mart   com*

    Luciae et Geminiani martyrum   com

17 Lamberti epi et mart   com

19 Sequani abbatis   com

20 Vigilia S. Mathei ap

21 MATHEI ap   XII

22 MAURITII CUM SOCIIS   XII

23   Teclae virg   com

24 Andochii, Tyrsi et Felicis martyrum   com

40
27 Cosmae et Damiani martyrum com*

29 MICHAELIS ARCHANGELI XII
41
30 IHERONOMI presbyteri XII

O C T O B E R

1 REMIGII ep XII

   Germani et Vedasti conf com   Replaced by: Vedasti et Amandi
                                                          42
                                              epp com

2 Leodegarii ep et mart com*

6   FIDIS virg et mart XII

7 Marci papae com

   Marcelli, Apulei, Sergii et Bachi mart com

9 DYONISII CUM SOCIIS SUIS XII Replaced by: DEDICATIO PARA-
                                                                43
                                   CLITENSIS ECCLESIAE XII

10   DYONISII CUM SOCIIS SUIS

                                   XII

14 Calixti papae et mart com*

18 LUCAE ev XII

21   NATALE UNDECIM MILIUM

                                        VIRG XII

25 Crispini et Crispiniani martyrum com

27 Vigilia Apostolorum Symonis et Iudae

28 NATALE APOSTOLORUM SYMONIS ET IUDAE   XII

29   CIRILLAE virg et mart

                                             XII

31 Vigilia Omnium Sanctorum

   Quintini mart   com

                    N O V E M B E R

1 FESTIVITAS OMNIUM SANCTORUM   XII

   Benigni et Ceasrii martyrum   com
                                  44
2 [Commemoratio omnium defunctorum]   EUSTACHII SOCIORUMQUE

                                           EIUS XII

8 Quattuor Coronatorum   com

9 Theodori mart   com

11 MARTINI ep XII

   Mennae mart   com

13 Brictii ep   com*

17 Aniani ep   com

18   Octavae S. Martini   com

21 Columbani abbatis   com

22 CAECILIAE virg et mart   XII

23 CLEMENTIS papae et mart   XII

   Sanctae Felicitatis   com

24 Grisogoni   mart   com

25   KATHERINAE virg et
                                                  45
                                     mart XII

27 Agricolae et Vitalis martyrum com

29 Vigilia Sancti Andreae

    Saturnini mart com

30 NATALE S. ANDREAE ap XII

DECEMBER

1 Crisanti, Mauri et Dariae com   ELIGII conf XII

6 NICHOLAI ep XII

    Octavae Sancti Andreae com

8   CONCEPTIO BVM XII

11 Damasi papae com

13 LUCIAE virg et mart XII

14   Nichasii sociorumque eius

                                           [com]

18   FLAVITI conf XII

21 THOMAE ap XII

24 Vigilia Natalis Domini

25 NATIVITAS DOMINI XII   Anastasiae mart com

                                     Eugeniae virg et mart
                                           46
                                     com

26 STEPHANI protomartyris XII

27 IOHANNIS ap et ev XII

28 SANCTORUM INNOCENTIUM XII

29   THOMAE archiep. cant.

                                     XII

31 SILVESTRI papae XII   Saviniani et Potentiani

                                     martyrum com

                                     Columbae virg com

In summary, there can be no reasonable doubt about it: the Paraclete calendar consists of the Cistercian calendar in its shape of around 1147, plus the celebrations retained from its antecedent calendar, or added in the course of the twelfth and thirteenth centuries.

THE CISTERCIAN "COLLECTANEUM"

This book has already been described above as the one with the Office collects and *capitula* or short readings. Though Dom Pierre Salmon has succeeded in identifying a number of early such manuscripts, and has traced the broad lines of the development of the later collectars or *collectanea* from simpler, earlier ninth-century forms,[47] no detailed study devoted to this book has yet appeared. Accordingly, it is more than difficult to situate the Cistercian *collectaneum* in its relationship to other traditions.

It is clear, however, that the collects included in this compilation are derived from the same unidentified sacramentary which supplied the prayers in the Mass book of the Order. In general, the medieval monastic Office was much more rich in Office collects than the Monastic Breviary of the post-Tridentine period. The collect of Prime and Compline varied from day to day only slightly, or not at all, but Sext and None each had its own proper collect on feasts and during the more important liturgical seasons; and the Matins collect was by no means invariably the same as the Lauds and Terce collect. Now, with no more than an astonishingly few exceptions, all the collects of the Cistercian Office are to be found in the edition of the *Gregorian Sacramentary* published by Dom Jean Deshusses in 1971.[48] Actually, the word 'sacramentary' in the preceding sentence is not quite correct, since Dom Deshusses has included in

his edition a number of different compilations which were used, at
different times and in different ways, in combination with the lacunose *Hadrianum ex authentico*. At my present stage of research,
it already seems quite clear that the Cistercian sacramentary--and
the corresponding collection of Office collects--are taken from an
exemplar with the following characteristics:

    1. The substance is drawn from a sacramentary of the 'Hadrian'
       type, but with a few formulas characteristic of the so-called
       Gregorianum Paduense;

    2. This material has been fused with formulas cribbed from the
       sacramentary *Supplementum* currently attributed by many litur-
       gists, who follow the lead of Dom Deshusses, to Benedict of
       Aniane;

    3. The remarkably few formulas which remain derive from one or
       more unidentified sources.

Since the elements of the *collectaneum* are included in any integral breviary manuscript, it is easy enough to follow the evolution of the Cistercian *collectaneum* from our earliest extant breviary
manuscript of around 1132 till the last part of the twelfth century.
Strictly speaking, changes are too slight to allow one to speak of a
real evolution. Whatever changes do occur result chiefly from additions or subtractions in the calendar.

THE PARACLETE "COLLECTANEUM"

    If we isolate the Office collects and *capitula* or short read-
ings from the rest of the material included in OBk, we find that we
have an absolutely complete *collectaneum*. We find, too, that it is
basically the Cistercian *collectaneum*. It follows the same history
of the calendar. The Cistercian *collectaneum* of the period around
1147 has been adopted *in toto*, but occasional material proper to
the Paraclete has been inserted here and there. Some of this material is of the highest interest, and the hand of Abelard can more than
once easily be identified, as in the following collect for the Feast
of St Philip, 'one of the Seven Deacons,' June 6:

    Deus, qui beatum Philippum diaconem sanctarum obsequio
    deputasti feminarum, te quaesumus: ut quem mensis earum
    delegasti ministrum, apud te semper habeamus patronum.
    Per.[49]

    It should not be thought, however, that every time the Para-
clete calendar has a Twelve Lesson Office or commemoration not found
in the Cistercian calendar, the corresponding section of OBk will
provide us with relics from the days of Abelard. More often than
not, this material is simply borrowed from the Cistercian Common.

THE CISTERCIAN ANTIPHONARY

In his Prologue to the Cistercian antiphonary revised under his own general direction around 1147, Bernard describes the basic attitude of the first Cistercians in terms of a passion for the 'authentic.'[50] In their chanting of the divine praises, they wished to sing only what was most authentic, only what had the guarantee of being covered by the most unimpeachable authority. In brief, this meant the antiphonary traditionally ascribed to Pope Saint Gregory the Great.[51] Modern scholarship has left us with precious few illusions about this mythical book of Office chants. In the less critical Middle Ages, however, no reader familiar with John the Deacon's *Life of Pope Saint Gregory* could be unaware of the fact that the ancient city of Metz was unrivalled in its fidelity to the most authentic gregorian chant tradition.[52] That things might have changed since the ninth century does not seem to have caused the early White Monks a great deal of concern. In their passion for the authentic, they went to Metz, found that the chant books there were not at all what they were expecting, but nevertheless copied them and used them for years--almost surely in virtue of the aura of 'authenticity' which still surrounded the Metz chant. But the second generation Cistercians seem to have been of less stern stuff than their immediate forebears. The time came, writes Bernard, when the brethren could no longer stand chanting such solemn nonsense day in and day out. ·The practical upshot was his appointment to supervise the revision of the texts and melodies of the books copied at Metz.[53]

No integral Cistercian chant manuscript of this early period is known to have survived. The Office antiphonary and Mass chantbook were among those manuscripts which required so many drastic changes that entirely new books had to be scrivened, and the old ones consigned to oblivion. However, by the careful study of erased and overwritten pre-1147 antiphonary folios which, providentially, have survived even to our own day, it is now possible to reconstruct major portions of the early Metz-Cistercian antiphonary.[54] It is easy enough to understand at long last why this Metz chant was thought to be so defective. The truth is that it really was pretty awful. For this there were two chief causes.

1. First of all, in the early twelfth century, the Metz scribes had to cope with the problem of the four-line staff. Heretofore, their melodies had been notated without much by way of clue as to precise pitch-relationships. The new-fangled invention of accurate melodic notation was still something of a novelty to such scribes, and the melodies were sometimes mutilated in this period of transition to notation on a staff.

2. Secondly, whatever might have been the glory of the Metz tradition at an earlier age, by the twelfth century this chant had

degenerated into a kind of 'chant dialect.' This is what often
happened in Germanic countries, where the cantors tended to raise
the pitches *mi* and *ti* to *fa* and *do* respectively--with disasterous
consequences for the standard form of the traditional melody.[55]
John the Deacon, who was inclined to be a bit prissy about the perfection of italianate singing compared with that of other lands,
has harsh things to say about his Teutonic brethren: 'Their coarse
voices, which roar like thunder, cannot execute soft modulations,
because their throats, hoarse from too much drinking, cannot emit
the inflexions required by a tender melody.'[56]

But even had the Metz melodies been truly representative of
the standard gregorian tradition at its best, there would still
have been a problem. For centuries theorists of music had been
busy studying the music of the Church, trying to understand its
shape and structure in such a way that all this could be expressed
in terms of music theory. It did not help matters that much of
this music theory was based on a profound misunderstanding of Greek
and Roman sources. Moreover, the chant which we dub 'gregorian'
had welled up with a life of its own, and without any help from
the theorists of music. When these traditional but--for the mathe-
matically inclined theorists--rather puzzling melodies clashed with
the inadequate principles formulated by the theorists, these learned men saw clearly that the fault lay on the part of the melodies,
rather than on the part of their own theorizing. The Cistercians
of Bernard's generation gave their total allegiance to the theorists. Perhaps this was a development of the 'reform mentality'
operative in the rise and early evolution of the Cistercian Order.
A thing was analyzed so that one could know what its inner nature
was. If it failed to conform with its real nature, it had to be
reformed. A few monks at Molesme had asked the questions: What
is an authentic monk? What is an authentic Benedictine monk? And
their practical response had been the foundation of Cîteaux. In
much the same way, the music theorists of Bernard's time, who asked themselves what music really ought to be, doubtless felt they
were simply being consistent when they decided to re-write the
Metz melodies not only to harmonize them with the standard chant
of their own region, but also to make them conform with the principles put forth by the theorists of music. One of the spokesman for
the Cistercian reformers admitted that the revised chant was now
different from all other versions. But this was a title to glory,
since, as he expressed it, what made Cistercian chant so different
was precisely *ratio.*[57]

This preoccupation with the reform of the melodies should not
make us lose sight of the fact, however, that the *texts* underwent
considerable revision, and, surely, in this domain no one would have
had more to contribute than Bernard. Material for these revisions
was furnished or suggested by a number of different liturgical books

collected precisely for this purpose--*de multis et diversis*58--but
often enough, the revised version of a given text seems to be a
specifically Cistercian contribution. Moreover, in spite of the
apparent preoccupation with the canons of music theory, the new
antiphonary integrated a sizable amount of material which, while
not precisely clashing with the older, more sober repertory, nevertheless breathed of a new spirit; and for this, we probably have
Bernard to thank. Finally, in spite of the systematic re-writing
of the Metz melodies on the basis of the principles formulated by
the theorists, in the last analysis, the antiphonary in its form
of around 1147 was much more in line with the traditional style of
chant than was the case of the chant dialect imported from Metz in
the early days of the Order.

THE PARACLETE ANTIPHONARY

Our manuscript of the Paraclete OBk contains not a single note
of chant. But even a superficial comparison of the antiphonary texts
of OBk with any post-1147 Cistercian antiphonary decides the question
in no uncertain terms: the Paraclete antiphonary was substantially
the same as the Cistercian model it obviously borrowed from. As for
the question of music, it would have been a practical impossibility
to have adopted the Cistercian texts without at the same time adopting their music.

But quite wonderful things remain from the earlier repertory;
and, as so often before, it is virtually impossible to ignore the
fact that the genius of Abelard has been at work. A series of Matins
invitatory antiphons, known only by their *incipits* in PO, and not
found outside the Paraclete, is probably the work of *le Mestre*, as
also a goodly number of responsories sung on special occasions. The
most massive *bloc* of non-Cistercian antiphonary material covers the
whole of Holy Week, beginning with First Vespers of Palm Sunday.
Antiphon texts are almost exclusively biblical, and are arranged in
such a way as, day by day, to follow the chronology of the events
of the first Holy Week. It becomes clear, the more one studies this
section of OBk, that the splendid series of proper hymns Abelard composed for Good Friday and Holy Saturday was only part of a much vas-
ter structure of his own creation. The Transfiguration Office, which
has only a few points of contact with the Orrice known to have been
composed by Peter the Venerable,59 might well have been composed by
Peter the Dialectician, for its inspiration is quite similar to that
of the Holy Week material proper to the Paraclete. But in addition
to those chants which can be ascribed to Abelard--though always ten-
tatively, and with the utmost caution--there have been retained from
the earlier Paraclete repertory a small number of 'old favorites'--
special antiphons and responsories known to have been immensely

popular and, in some instances, a bit on the extravagant side.

In spite of these two groups of non-Cistercian material, however, even a hasty analysis of the antiphonary texts shows that the Paraclete Office was created by simply taking the Cistercian antiphonary of the Bernardine type, and by interpolating into it (and, in a few instances, substituting) material retained from the earlier Paraclete tradition.

Special note should be taken of the 'Cistercian features' of the Office structure. In spite of so many proper texts of Abelard in the Sacred Triduum Offices, the structure of these is that of a weekday in Passiontide. This is a bit ironic, because Peter, in his *Letter 10* to Bernard, had made a special point of this Cistercian novelty, since it went clean contrary to the long-established monastic usage of adopting the Roman Office for the last three days of Holy Week.[60] He had also had harsh things to say about the retention of *Alleluia* in the Office between Septuagesima and Lent, even though the Holy Rule drops this sign of paschal joy only as of the beginning of Lent.[61] Still, Heloise and her nuns have adopted the Cistercian practice. The same type of literalism had led the Cistercians to chant Alleluia-antiphons on Sundays in Advent and Christmastide, rather than the proper seasonal antiphons used elsewhere, and to chant all the psalms of Lauds under a single antiphon. So also at the Paraclete.

In spite of the absence of most of the Matins texts in OBk, there are indications that Matins at the Paraclete had been 'cistercianized' along with the rest of the Hours. The occasional chant *incipits* given in PO are generally those of the Cistercian Office, and the weekday antiphons series, written out *in extenso* in OBk, is the characteristic Cistercian one. In the instance of a number of feast day Offices, the four antiphons of Second Vespers enable one to reconstruct the first part of the Matins series of antiphons. It was a widespread practice to borrow the antiphons of Second Vespers from the Matins series, and, in the case of the Paraclete books, and Vespers antiphons are identical with the first four antiphons of the Cistercian Night Office series. There is a reference to an Easter Matins series of responsories which is probably by Abelard, and we can be confident that he provided still other Matins material which managed to survive at the Paraclete for many centuries. But the evidence points in the direction of a substantially Cistercian-style Matins.

The Cistercian antiphonary underwent only very minor changes after the drastic revision of around 1147, and, so far as we know, these changes were introduced progressively from around 1175 onwards. The Cistercian material identifiable in the Paraclete manuscripts belongs to the 1147-1175 period, which is also the case of the calendar, the *collectaneum*, and--one would think--the hymnal. But the study of the Cistercian hymnbook at the Paraclete leads to a surprisingly different conclusion.

THE CISTERCIAN HYMNAL

In four separate passages of his *Holy Rule* **Benedict** uses the technical term *ambrosianum* to stand for *hymnus*.[62] Since exegetes of the *Rule* understood *ambrosianum* to mean a hymn composed by St Ambrose himself--though this, they agreed, was only one of several possible interpretations[63]--the first Cistercians, in keeping with their passion for the authentic, and in virtue of their absolute fidelity to the *Rule* as they understood it, adopted whatever was usable in the Milanese hymnbook. Though the Milanese repertory of the early twelfth century gives signs of a certain amount of evolution, its archaic character nevertheless is striking. Hymns are relatively few, and only a single Vigils (that is to say, Matins) hymn is provided. This distinctive hymnbook provided Abelard with ample material for his catalogue of Cistercian liturgical oddities in *Letter 10*. He rightly accuses the White Monks of having outlawed familiar tunes and texts in favor of hymns for the most part unknown in home regions; the same **Vigils** humn was sung daily, feast or fast, in season and out of season, and the number of hymns was so small that they failed to cover all the exigencies of the liturgical cycle.[64] An initial timid response to this criticism may be seen in a pre-1147 hymnal insert bound with a Clairvaux breviary of a later date.[65] The Milanese hymnbook had usually provided only a single hymn for the major feasts, and this the Cistercians had sung at First and Second Vespers, and at Lauds, while the sempiternal *Aeterne rerum Conditor* remained attached to Matins. In our Clairvaux insert, divisions have been introduced in most of these Vespers hymns, so that the hymns could now be sung in this manner: at both sets of Vespers, the integral hymn was sung; at Matins, the first division; and at Lauds, the second. This practice, of course, had a monotony of its own, but it was less deadening than the earlier practice. The reform of around 1147 provided a much better solution to the problem of the hymns. Bernard must have noticed that, though Benedict does use the term *ambrosianum*, he does so only with reference to Matins, Lauds, and Vespers. The way was thus opened for the introduction of non-Ambrosian hymns at the other Hours, with the result that the familiar, tried and true regional repertory jettisoned by the first White Monks now reappeared at Terce and Compline. The Milanese melodies were systematically revised in keeping with the ideas of the theorists, and in some instances completely new, freshly composed Cistercian tunes were substituted for the little loved and poorly understood archaic Milanese melodies. The noted hymnologist, Bruno Stäblein, has identified ten, perhaps eleven melodies in the old Cistercian hymnbook as specifically cistercian-authored.[66] I myself can make out a good case only for eight.[67] But what glorious melodies! The chant theory of the Cistercian musicians was admittedly a bit unfortunate, but those anonymous Cistercian theorists surely knew how to create melodies of incomparable excellence.

THE PARACLETE HYMNAL

Thanks to several editions of Abelard's hymns during the last and present centuries,[68] the hymnographical work of Master Peter is well known and rightly appreciated. No less than 133 hymns are included in his collection, which is divided into three *libelli*, each of which has its own instructive Preface.

In his Preface to the first *libellus*,[69] Peter puts into Heloise's mouth the arguments against many of the traditional hymns. She claims that too many of these hymns are sung according to 'custom,' and 'authority' is not followed. Her meaning—which seems to have been misunderstood by the many commentators on this text—is that too many of the standard hymns are anonymous, and therefore are without authority. For a hymn to be authentic or authoritative, it had to come down from an acknowledged authority. She explains her thought by the parallel case of the so-called 'Gallican Psalter,' translated by no one knew whom. It was nevertheless the standard psalter for liturgical use, even though there was readily at hand the Latin translation of the Hebrew psalter by that authority of authorities, St Jerome. In Heloise's mind, and in keeping with the categories of Abelard's thought, the Gallican psalter had custom behind it, but not authority. So, too, in the case of many hymns. The argument continues. Granted that we *do* know the authors of many hymns—Hilary, Ambrose, Prudentius, and still others—their texts, though authoritative, are no true hymns. Why? Because, according to a standard definition of 'hymn,' a hymn is *laus Dei cum cantico*, whereas many of these authoritative texts are quite unsingable. But why are they unsingable? Because: *tanta est frequenter inaequalitas syllabarum, ut vix cantici melodiam recipiant.*[70] Here again the commentators have missed the meaning. Heloise is speaking about the problems created in the ancient texts by reason of the presence of elisions. By counting two syllables as one, the classical writers managed to keep their metrical or rhythmical patterns in order. But, by the time of the twelfth century, the use of elision in the venerable hymn texts seems to have been little understood. One must look long and hard to find a single elision in Abelard's 133 hymns. As an example of what Heloise is complaining about, consider Stanza Five of the Milanese hymn for St John the Evangelist, *Amore Christi nobilis*. In theory, the structure allows for eight syllables in each line: 8 - 8 - 8 - 8, but Heloise would have counted, and sung (or tried to sing): 9 - 9 - 10 - 9.

> *In principio erat Verbum,*
> *Et Verbum erat apud Deum;*
> *Et Deus erat Verbum, hoc erat*
> *In principio apud Deum.*

Unfortunately, the Cistercian hymns imported from Milan abounded in such texts. The White Monks, too, had difficulty reconciling the hymn melodies with texts which refused to remain regular, syllable-wise, from line to line. This is why so many of the early Cistercian hymnbooks with chant notation present each stanza of most hymns with full melodic notation. The monks *must* have understood the principles of elision well enough, schooled as many of them were in the dangerous splendors of classical Latin poetry, but the evidence shows that they refused to chant a ten-syllable line as an eight-syllable line, even though the rhythmic pattern called for only eight syllables.

Heloise similarly complains that 'authoritative' hymns are too few to meet the needs of the entire liturgical year. Then, too, there was the problem of what modern liturgists call *veritas horarum*. The very texts of certain hymns attach them to certain periods of the day or night. Heloise pointed out that many a hymn originally destined for night use, was being sung at the wrong time, due to the exigences of the pastoral ministry and a changed tempo of life. Finally, so many of these hymn texts were couched in terms of such unrealistic hyperbole, that it was hard to take them seriously.71

The response to Heloise's criticism was Abelard's own hymnbook. The first *libellus* contained a complete series of hymns for Sunday and weekday use throughout the year. The second *libellus* was devoted chiefly to hymns for Feasts of the Lord. And the third *libellus* supplied hymns for feasts of Our Lady and other saints. The Preface to *Libellus III* suggests that Peter felt free to treat the liturgical prescriptions of the Benedictine *Rule* with a rather light touch. On feast days, not one, but *three* hymns are provided for Matins, so that each of the three Nocturns or divisions of the Night Office can have its own proper hymn. Thus three hymns, plus the single Lauds hymn, provide a group of four which may be sub-grouped in such a way that the first two hymns are sung at First Vespers, the last two at Second Vespers. Peter suggests yet another arrangement of the Vespers hymns, in which the first would be grouped with the first two psalms, and the second with the last two psalms.72 Presumably, Bernard's visit to the Paraclete took place before the introduction of Peter's hymnbook; otherwise he would have had more to startle him than the change of a single word in the traditional Office version of the Lord's Prayer.

In the light of the results earlier obtained by a comparison of Cistercian Official material with the corresponding formulas of the Paraclete material, we know what to expect: We shall find the Cistercian hymnbook of the 1147 type, plus a sprinkling of Abelard's better efforts. But, no, this is *not* what we find to be the case.

The first surprise to meet us is this: about one third of Abelard's hymns have been excluded from OBk. Most of the utterly perfect hymns of the Sunday Office fortunately remain, but the

weekday cycle has vanished *in toto*, and the minuscule series of
Cistercian weekday hymns has taken its place. In *Libelli II* and
III, the pruning has been more moderate. Still, out of 133 hymns,
some thirty-nine have been eliminated.

The second surprise is this: all the hymn texts of the primitive Milano-Cistercian hymnal are to be found in OBk. A superficial analysis might create the initial impression that the Cistercian hymnal represented is that of the Bernardine revision, since
a number of the hymns introduced into this hymnal by Bernard are
also in the Paraclete books. But if we compare the Cistercian
and Paraclete versions of *Conditor alme siderum, Vexilla regis pro-
deunt*, and others of this same group, we find the textual variants
so many and so serious, that we have to admit of a third *bloc* of
hymns at the Paraclete. These hymns owe nothing to either Abelard
or to Cîteaux, and come from some unidentified source or sources.

In summary, at this stage of the analysis, we must recognize
three distinct groups of hymns in the Paraclete repertory:

Group I: A hymn *corpus* of about two-third's of Peter's hymns;
Group II: The pre-1147 Cistercian hymn texts;
Group III: Hymns from other sources.

In Group III, the only hymns from a late date are the Corpus
Christi series, obviously adopted in the late thirteenth or early
fourteenth century. But the remaining hymns provide for Advent,
Lent, Passiontide, and Trinity Sunday--precisely those seasons and
that feast for which we find nothing in Peter's hymnbook. But then,
Peter never said he intended to write a complete hymnbook. And if
he wrote hymns only for the Sunday and weekday cycle, for feasts of
the Lord, and for feasts of Mary and the other saints, it was probably because the seasonal hymn chants already in the Paraclete repertory managed to pass muster. Another point which is based on no more
than an informed guess: when Peter has Heloise complain, in his Preface to *Libellus I*, about the inadequacies of those hymns which enjoy
great authority, but are nevertheless unsingable and insufficient for
the demands of the liturgical year, she can be describing only one
hymn *corpus*--the Milano-Cistercian hymnbook. This collection of ancient hymn texts is found in the Paraclete liturgy of the early fourteenth century. It must have been current at the Paraclete even *before* Bernard's reform, for, after 1147, the nuns would surely have
adopted the revised version, along with the Cistercian calendar, *collectaneum*, and antiphonary.

*A CAUTIOUS FIRST ATTEMPT AT A SYNTHESIS: THE GENETIC
HISTORY OF THE EARLY PARACLETE OFFICE*

1. In the earliest days after the installation of Heloise and
her nuns at the Paraclete, the hymns would have been simply those

of the traditional repertory of the region. At this critical period
in the life of the nascent nunnery, Abelard claims to have held himself pretty much aloof--which was not difficult, considering the
fact that he was at that time the long-suffering abbot of Saint-
Gildas de Rhuys in distant Brittany.[73] It was during this time of
beginnings that Heloise proved her mettle. 'Bishops loved her as a
daughter, abbots as a sister, the laity as their mother.'[74] Was Bernard one of those abbots who loved Heloise as a sister? We know for
sure of at least one visit of his to the Paraclete. Was this visit
followed up by further help of a practical nature?--help which might
have extended so far as aiding Heloise to organize the liturgical
life of her community? It would be rash to answer 'Yes.' Still, if
the early Cistercian hymnbook found its way to the Paraclete, it was
quite possibly at this early date. Consider, too, Abelard's remarkable inside knowledge of the Cistercian Office of this time. Orderi-
cus Vitalis, writing just a few years later about the strange new
breed of monks, tells us that the Cistercians allowed only their own
monks in choir.[75] Surely there were exceptions to this practice,
and perhaps Abelard was one such exception. But even a somewhat extended visit to a Cistercian monastery of the period would have net-
ted even the sharp-eyed Abelard much less practical knowledge than
he evinces when he describes particular points of Cistercian usage
in his *Letter 10*. It is possible, just possible, that Abelard's
first-hand contact with this liturgy took place at the Paraclete,
where Heloise and her community had not only a Cistercian hymnal,
but a copy of the Usages and other manuscripts useful for shaping
up a liturgy along Cistercian lines.

    2. 'I began to visit them quite often to help them in any way
I could,' writes Abelard.[76] One of the areas where he helped in a
most signal way was that of their liturgy. He tossed together a
collection of his sermons for reading in refectory and before Com-
pline--and the frequent references to this *Book of Master Peter's
Sermons* in PO is proof that the sermons were still staple community fare in the later thirteenth century. He also composed an enormous hymn repertory for their use, and the Abelardian remains still
to be found in the 'cistercianized' Paraclete books of a much later
period suggest that his contribution by way of special Offices and
antiphons and responsories was considerably more important than
heretofore has been suspected. It was to help Heloise, too, that
he wrote his *Problemata Heloissae*;[77] and his commentary on the *Hex-
aemeron* was likewise written in answer to the request of the Paraclete community.[78] Most important of all, however, is the dossier
of letters exchanged between Peter and Heloise. I personally feel
that the preoccupation of historians with the initial *Letter of
Consolation,* and the romanticists' interest only in the next four
letters, which are of a rather intimate nature, have long made it
difficult to see clearly that, as John Benton has so well pointed

out,[79] this collection of letters forms a single unity. The story
of the conversion of the lovers to a new and deeper union in the
religious life simply sets the stage for Abelard, whose intention
it is to become Father Founder of a somewhat new form of religious
life. Benedict had his Scholastica, Francis was to have his Clare,
and François de Sales his Jeanne de Chantal. But for the mysterious
workings of the grace of God, Peter and Heloise might have been added to the list. Double monasteries were hardly a novelty by the time
of the twelfth century, of course;[80] and it would be difficult to
identify, in the structures described by Peter in his *Institutio seu
Regula sanctimonialium*--that is to say, his *Letter 8*[81]--anything particularly distinctive when compared with the structures of the double-
community which grew up under the direction of Stephen at Obazine.[82]
Where Peter's fantasy runs a bit wild, however, is where he fills in
these structures with his highly personal ideas about the ideal monastic community. He wants this community to incarnate the purest form
of primitive Christianity. But he is also obsessed with his own role
as a St Jerome *redivivus*, and Heloise inevitably finds herself cast
in the corresponding role of Paula or Asella. For the student of
monastic institutions, *Letter 8* is a tremendously exciting document.
Only one wonders to what extent it was ever actually implemented.
At any rate, I do not think it at all rash to suggest that, from the
time Peter began showing an active interest in life at the Paraclete,
he influenced the shape of their community prayer to so great an extent that, even after a subsequent 'cistercianization' of the Office,
the initial Abelardian contribution managed to survive, albeit in
fragmented form.

     3. A comparison of the Paraclete material with the Cistercian
Office texts and chants shows a virtual identity between the two for
the period running roughly from around 1147 to around 1175/1180;
and, certainly, the Paraclete was dependent on Cîteaux, rather than
vice versa. Sometime after 1147, then, the Cistercian Office was
adopted by the nuns, though with the retention of a certain amount
of material from the time of Abelard.

     But since every effect has to have its proportionate cause, why
did the nuns of the Paraclete abandon their earlier Office books in
favor of the Cistercian Office? There is absolutely no indication
that these nuns ever developed an anti-Abelard bias--quite the contrary! And, after the Council of Sens, I dare say that it must have
taken an uncommon amount of Christian virtue on their part not to
look at Bernard and the White Monks with a somewhat jaundiced eye.
Insisting on the fact that the following remarks represent no more
than working hypotheses, I should like to draw attention to these
points:

     1. Soon after the death of Abelard in 1142,[83] the Paraclete
began swarming. By the time of Heloise's own death in 1164, and
perhaps by as early as 1157,[84] colonies of Paraclete nuns had

founded new communities—La Pommeraie, Sainte-Madeleine de Trainel,
Laval-les-Lagny, Noéfort, and Saint-Flavit.[85] The Paraclete was now
head of a Congregation. As this expansion began to take place, it
was all but inevitable that the Paraclete program of monastic observance be passed in review, since no one would have thought of following in a daughter-house a form of observance much different from that
of the mother-house. Providentially, we have from this period of
initial expansion an extremely precious document which only now seems
to be attracting the attention it has long deserved. I refer to the
Paraclete Rule edited by F. d'Amboise in the *editio princeps* of Abelard's works, under the title which still appears in the Migne re-
edition—*Excerpta ex regulis Paracletensis monasterii.*[86] The historical context in which this brief, practical Rule was redacted can
easily be gathered from one of the early sections of the document:[87]

> Domino super nos prospiciente, et aliqua loca
> nobis largiente, misimus quasdam ex nostris
> ad religionem tenendam numero sufficiente.
> Annotamus autem boni propositi nostri con-
> suetudines, ut quod tenuit mater incommuta-
> biliter, teneant et filiae uniformiter.

This squares wonderfully well with what we read in the charter
of Hugh, archbishop of Sens, for the first foundation of La Pommeraie,
in 1147 at the latest: *Alium ordinem, nisi Paraclitensem, non liceb-
it eis observare.*[88]

We have then, a Paraclete mini-Rule remarkable for its simplicity, clarity, and lack of fussiness. It is also remarkable for the
fact that, in a number of important features, it is absolutely incompatible with the long spiritual directory and Rule for nunneries
which passes as Abelard's *Letter 8*. Whether this Rule in *Letter 8*
was ever observed at the Paraclete, and, if so, to what extent—
these are problems which admit of no sure answer. What is quite
certain, on the basis of present evidence, is that the Paraclete
had been deeply influenced by the presence and activity of Peter
Abelard. This is evident even in the much revised liturgy of a
later period. But surely this omni-presence of Abelard at the Paraclete posed something of a practical problem, expecially after the
trauma of his condemnation at Sens in 1140. How many bishops would
be particularly happy to accept into their dioceses communities of
nuns with a special *cultus* of Abelard, their saintly Founding Father?
And was it really possible to transplant elsewhere all the particu-
larisms and somewhat exotic features of the Paraclete of the early
days?

Then, too, the Abelardian *liturgica* which have survived point
in the direction of a somewhat different problem. It would be all
impossible to praise too highly Peter's literary gifts and theological depth of understanding. But there is no denying the fact that

most of his extant compositions are virtuoso pieces. His hymns
teem with imagination, and the lofty standard of his poetic skill
maintains itself stanza after stanza. But in a monastic liturgy,
verbal pyrotechnics go a long way, and a steady diet of Abelard's
astonishing feats of composition would be a bit like dining on
chocolate mousse six times a week. It is significant that the
bulk of the many hymns dropped from Peter's hymnbook include most
of the ferial day cycle, which came in for rather frequent repeti-
tion. Unfortunately, the twenty-nine hymns included in *Libellus I*
admitted of only two metrical patterns -- 8 - 8 - 10 - 10 and 12 -
12 - 12 - 12, with only two corresponding melodies.[89] What was
needed was something rather more neutral, something which could
be repeated often, and yet wear well.

Whatever the proximate occasion for the adoption of so much
Cistercian material, I think that, all things considered, the
choice was one which was well thought out. And if it is true that
this change in liturgical practice came about in the context of
the Paraclete foundations, then it was Heloise who bore the chief
responsibility for this decision. She was a great woman, a *very*
great woman. Whatever her personal feelings towards Bernard might
have been after the Council held at Sens, she remained *la très sage
Héloïse*. If the circumstances brought about by the sudden multi-
plication of foundations seemed to call for a 'de-abelardization'
of the unique Paraclete liturgy, the White Monks certainly had a
great deal to offer by way of a replacement. In matters liturgical
they were the touch-stone of orthodoxy. No bishop need fear being
responsible for nunneries with so sensible a Rule and so Cistercian
an approach to the celebration of the Divine Office. Further, it
might well be that Abelard's ideals were better achieved by the
White Monks than by Abelard himself, despite his raillery against
them with respect chiefly to points of minor importance. The Cistercian liturgy was based essentially on a passion for the authentic, but it also extolled the principle of *ratio* almost beyond
reasonable measure. At the same time, the Cistercian Office as
reformed under Bernard's aegis managed to combine sobriety with
lyricism, reserve with exuberance, classical values with the spirit of the age of trouvère and troubador. More than one musicolo-
gist has noted the identity of inspiration and spirit between one
of the few of Abelard's melodies we possess--the glorious hymn-
tune, *O quanta qualia*--and the Cistercian-composed hymn tunes of
the bernardine hymnbook.[90]

Heloise need not have turned to clairvaux for the liturgical
Office books of the Bernardine reform. Without being juridically
incorporated into the Order, the nuns of nearby Tart were Cistercian through and through, and there were other Cistercian nunneries and monasteries which could easily have supplied material for
copying.

However, most of this is simply guess-work, and might risk obscuring the essential point of this paper, which is too solidly established by the manuscript evidence to admit of much question. For, beyond all doubt, the Paraclete manuscripts of the late thirteenth and early fourteenth century are proof that, at some time in the distant past, the earlier Paraclete Office had been all but replaced by the Cistercian Office reformed by the man whom Abelard once called *amicum, immo amicissimum*—Bernard of Clairvaux.

Abbey of Gethsemani

NOTES

1. See the *Chronicon Mauriniacensis monasterii, Lib.II*, towards
   the end; in MGH SS 26, pp. 40–41; or, under the title *Teulfi
   Chronicon Mauriniacense*, in PL 180:159 C.

2. GCh 12, *Instrumenta*, p. 259; PL 179:114; Charles Lalore, *Cartulaire de l'abbaye du Paraclet [Collection des principaux cartulaires du diocèse de Troyes*, 2] (Paris, 1878) p. 1.   Other
   editions noted in Jaffé-Lowenfeld, *Regesta Pontificum Romanorum*
   (Leipzig, 1885) I, 852, n. 7513 (5386). The text is referred
   to under the date November 28, and Auxerre is given as the
   place where Innocent II issued this privilege.

3. Scholars are no longer in general agreement as to the identification of the 'new Apostles...one of whom claimed it as his
   glory that he had revived the life of Canons Regular, the other
   that of monks' (Abelard, *Ad amicum suum consolatoria epistola*,
   p. 202 of the edition by J. T. Muckle, in *Mediaeval Studies* 12
   [1950]; PL 178:164 A). If Bernard--heretofore identified as
   the monkish villain in Abelard's text--is *not* to be identified
   as Peter's adversary at this time, then most of the evidence
   converges to suggest that the two monks began as friends. For
   a brief discussion and bibliography on the question of the
   earlier contacts between the two, see Chrysognous Waddell,
   in John R. Sommerfeldt (ed.), *Studies in Medieval Cistercian
   History*, II [CS 24] pp. 75–86.

4. PL 178:335–340. The *editio princeps* of 1616, begun by François
   d'Amboise, but completed by André Duchesne, begins a new series
   of letters after the Abelard-Heloise series, and, in this new
   series--*Aliae Mag[istri] Petri Abaelardi Nannetensis Epistolae*--
   our *Letter 10* appears as *Epistola V*.

5. PL 178:335 BC.

6. Text edited by Jean Leclercq, *Etudes sur S. Bernard et le texte
   de ses écrits* (ASOC 9; Rome, 1953) pp. 104–105; and by R. Kli-
   bansky, 'Peter Abailard and Bernard of Clairvaux: A Letter by
   Abailard,' *Medieval and Renaissance Studies* 5 (1961) 22–32.
   Also edited in part by J. T. Muckle, in the Appendix to his
   edition of Abelard's *Letter of Consolation to a Friend*, in *Mediaeval Studies* 12 (1950) 213.

7. PL 178:335 B.

8. See the article by C. Waddell, referred to above, Footnote 3.

9. For a brief description of some of the surviving manuscripts of the early period, see Chrysogonus Waddell, 'The Early Cistercian Experience of Liturgy,' in M. Basil Pennington (ed.), *Rule and Life: A Symposium* (CS 12) pp. 94-95, with special reference to the footnotes.

10. Extant manuscripts of the *Vita beati Stephani abbatis monasterii Obazinensis*, written in the second half of the twelfth century by an anonymous disciple of the father founder of Obazine, give only an abridged form of the long text first edited by Etienne Baluze in 1683. The text was reprinted in the Author's *Miscellanea* 1 (Lucca, 1761). The text important for our present discussion is found in Chapter 13 of Book II, p. 161 of the Lucca edition. Even the recent critical edition by Michel aubrun, *Vie de saint Etienne d'Obazine: Texte et traduction* (*Publication de l'Institut d'études du Massif Central*, fasc. 6; Clermont-Ferrand, 1970) has had to borrow from Baluze in order to establish the integral text of this important Cistercian biography.

11. *Vita beati Stephani*, Lib. III, cap. 13: 'Itaque alios [libros] in ipsis a fundamentis incipiebant, alios radebant et denuo rescribebant, alios ex integro demittebant, alios paucis immutatis sibi iterum retinebant.'

12. *Ibid.*: 'Sed sciendum quod libri quibus primo Cistercienses in divinis officiis usi sunt, valde corrupti ac vitiosi fuerunt....'

13. *Ibid.*: '...Et usque ad tempora sancti Bernardi permanserunt. Tunc enim Abbatum communi decreto ab eodem sancto Abbate ejusque cantoribus sunt correcti et emendati, et sicut modo habentur dispositi.'

14. *Op. S. Bern.*, 3: 511-16, with special reference to p. 515; also in PL 182:1121-22.

15. *Ibid.*: 'Ego vero, accitis de ipsis fratribus nostris [the antecedent is: iam fratribus nostris abbatibus ordinis], qui in arte et usu canendi instructiores atque peritiores inventi sunt....'

16. Guy's *curriculum vitae* would include a period spent at Eu, near Rouen (texts refer to him as *Guido augiensis*); a few years as novice and young monk at Clairvaux, where he had William--later first abbot of Rievaulx--as novice master and where he wrote the treatise *Regulae de arte musica*, edited by E. de Coussemaker in an impossibly bad version, in *Scriptores de Musica Medii Aevi*, Nova Series 2 (Paris, 1857); and, finally, the greater part of his monastic life as abbot of Cherlieu.

17. Paris, Bibliothèque nationale, MS français 14410.

18. This type of liturgical book has been variously designated
     under an extraordinarily large number of different names—
     *Ordinarius, Ordinarium, Ordinale, Ordo officiorum, Breve,
     Rubrica, Directorium chori*, etc. For a more extended list
     of equivalent terms, see Adalbert Kurzeja, *Der älteste* Liber
     Ordinarius *der Trierer Domkirche: Liturgiewissenschaftliche
     Quellen und Forschungen* 52 (Münster Westfalen, 1970) pp. 1–2,
     with special reference to footnote 3, p. 2. A comprehensive
     bibliography of printed editions of *Libri Ordinarii* is given
     in Anton Hänggi, *Der Rheinauer Liber Ordinarius* (Freiburg
     [Schweiz], 1957) pp. XXIV–XXXVI. The Paraclete Ordinal is
     now being edited for publication.

19. A good example is the synod statute of Bishop Nicholas Gelant
     of Angers, for the year 1261: 'Statuimus quod in singulis
     Ecclesiis liber, qui dicitur Ordinarius, habeatur quo Sacer-
     dotes respiciant singulis diebus ante vesperarum inceptionem,
     ut ipsas vesperas, matutinas et officium diei sequentis faci-
     ant et exequantur, juxta Ordinarii institutionem.' Text first
     edited by Luc d'Achéry, *Veterum aliquot scriptorum...spici-
     legium* (Paris, 1723) I, 726.

20. Ff. 1–28. The best and most recent edition is to be found in
     the series *Receuil des historiens de la France: Obituaires de
     la Province de Sens* 4 (Diocèses de Meaux et de Troyes) (Paris,
     1923), 'Abbaye du Paraclet,' pp. 387–430. The earlier edi-
     tion by Charles Lalore, *Collection des principaux obituaires et
     confraternités du diocèse de Troyes* (Paris, 1882) pp. 446–60,
     is rather poor.

21. Chaumont, Bibliothèque municipale, MS 31. Whereas PO contains
     no reference to a Corpus Christi Office, this manuscript con-
     tains a complete office for this feast (apart from the omission
     of Matins)—the same Office as the popular one based on the sec-
     ular, rather than monastic *cursus*, and which became current soon
     after 1264. No attempt has been made to harmonize this Office
     with the monastic form of Office; so that First Vespers is as-
     signed five antiphons, as in the Roman Office, rather than four,
     as in the monastic Office. At the time our manuscript was writ-
     ten, the Corpus Christi Office was still enough of a novelty to
     justify the scribe's using for his rubrical introduction, f.
     110r: 'Incipit officium noue sollempnitatis eucharistie.' For
     a summary treatment of the origins and rapid spread of this par-
     ticular Corpus Christi Office, see Joseph Pascher, *Das litur-
     gische Jahr* (München, 1963) pp. 269–72.

22. For a brief history of the stages which led up to the appearance of the modern type breviary, see Pierre Salmon, *L'Office divin au Moyen Age (Lex Orandi* 43; Paris, 1967).

23. For the approximate dates of St Robert's *curriculum vitae*, see Kolomban Spahr, *Das Leben des hl. Robert von Molesme: Eine Quelle zur Vorgeschichte vox Cîteaux* (Freiburg in der Schweiz, 1944) pp. xliii-xlvii; of even [with a few minor corrections], Jacques Laurent, *Cartulaires de l'abbaye de Molesme* (Paris, 1907) I, 146-53.

24. For the Montier-la-Celle calendar, we have Troyes, Bibliothèque municipale, MS 1974, from the late thirteenth century--a breviary without chant notation; from the same library, MS 109-- a winter season breviary with full chant notation. MS 360, of the Bibliothèque municipale of Chalons-sur-Marne, is too lacunose and too much interpolated with late material to be used without a great deal of caution. For the Molesme calendar, we have the mid-twelfth-century summer season breviary, now classified in the Bibliothèque municipale of Troyes as MS 807; and though Evreux, Bibiolthèque municipale, MS 124 is a composite manuscript with non-Molesmian material, the calendar, given *in extenso*, is that of Molesme.

25. This important manuscript provides us with an integral breviary of the pre-1147 period. Acquired by the Preussische Staats-Bibliothek of Berlin during World War II, the manuscript was later transferred to Marburg a.d. Lahn, and classified as MS lat. in octavo 402. The manuscript is now back in West Berlin. The long awaited edition of the text, edited by Abbot Kassien Lauterer of Mehrerau, will appear in the series *Bibliotheca Cisterciensis*, Editiones Cistercienses, Rome. The calendar of around 1132 appears *in extenso*, ff. 1v-7r, with *computus*-tables added, f. 7v.

26. Like the Cistercians, the early Camaldolese monks seem to have recognized only Twelve Lesson feasts and commemorations in their calendar. See the facsimile edition of the ancient Camaldolese antiphonary, Lucca, Biblioteca capitolare, MS 601, in *Paléographie musicale* (Tournai, 1906) IX, 18*-20*, for tables of the Sanctoral Offices, with the structure of each outlined; pp. 43*-56*, for a discussion of the particularities of this primitive sanctoral cycle, with special reference to p. 48*, where the absence of Three Lesson feasts is treated briefly. A superficial glance at the earliest extant Carthusian calendar of around 1134, reproduced in DACL 3/1, 1051-52, might create the impression that the Carthusians, too, had no Three Lesson

feasts. But such feasts were included, in point of fact, among the four degrees of feasts characteristic of the Order from its earliest days. References to these feasts are frequent in the several ancient redactions of the Carthusian customaries edited by James Hogg, *Die ältesten* Consuetudines *der Kartäuser (Analecta Cartusiana* 1; 1970).

27. The breviary as described above, note 25. The sacramentaries are: Paris, Bibliothèque nationale, MS lat. 2300; and Reims, Bibliothèque municipale, MS 310. Two evangeliaries: Colmar, Bibliothèque municipale, MS 107; and Paris, Bibliothèque nationale, MS lat. 1128. So far I have been able to identify only a single epistolary dating from the same early period: Laon, Bibliothèque municipale, MS 248.

28. Sts Caesarius and Benignus were expunged from November 1 at an unspecified date before 1180; St Bernard was introduced in 1174, and assigned a proper Office in 1175; in the same year the Holy Trinity Office was adopted, in a version stylistically much the same as the Paraclete version, which doubtless was celebrated at the Paraclete from an early date: the oratory originally had been dedicated in honor of the Trinity, as Abelard attests, and as the earliest Paraclete charters attest also. Because of a mis-interpretation of Statute 36 of the General Chapter of 1185, it has long been thought that the feast of St Thomas Becket was adopted in that year, but the statute in question deals only with the number of conventual Masses to be celebrated on this day, and pre-supposes that the feast was already in the calendar—and this it was by around 1180. In a twelfth/thirteenth century manuscript now at Laon, Bibliothèque municipale, MS 471, f. 102v, Fr Jean Leclercq discovered a list of *statuta* of the General Chapter of 1182, and among these *statua*   is a reference to a recent revision of a number of the Order's liturgical books: 'Lectionarium, Missale, Textus, Epistolare, Collectaneum nuper emendata sunt.' See Fr Leclercq's article, 'Epîtres d'Alexandre III sur les Cisterciens,' R Ben 64 (1954) 77.

29. See, for instance, the entry for January 29, St Gildas, patron of the rugged Breton abbey where Abelard spent a number of years as the hard-pressed and persecuted abbot of the community; or September 3, St Ayoul, the patron of the priory in which Abelard found haven after his precipitous flight from St Denis.

30. A *vigilia* entry in the Cistercian calendar could well be expected, since the Vigil of Epiphany did call for a special Office collect.

31. The OBk calendar indicates a separate commemoration for these two saints, but f. 132r of the MS, as well as f. 71r of PO, prove that both saints are included in a single commemoration.

32. Rank of celebration omitted in OBk calendar, but supplied from the body of the same MS, f. 132c; also from PO, f. 71r, as well as f. 123r of the *Processionale*. This latter portion of the manuscript is an invaluable aid to the identification of Twelve Lesson feasts, since, so often as these fell on a Sunday, there was always a special chant sung in their honor at the usual Sunday morning procession through the cloister. Simple commemorations received no mention in the *Processionale*. Accordingly, explicit mention of a saint in this Ordinary for Processions is an indication that the saint was accorded a Twelve Lesson celebration.

33. PO, f. 79v solves the obvious impossibility of having two Twelve Lesson feasts on the same day, by transferring St Thibaut to the following day.

34. The scribe of the OBk calendar had three entries to squeeze in for a single day, August 1. Though it might look as if St Eusebius belongs to August 2, f. 167r of OBk proves otherwise; so also PO, f. 82r.

35. It is curious that the pre-1147 calendar of the Landais sacramentary, Bibliothèque nationale, MS lat. 2300, also contains an entry for these two schoolboy martyrs from Alcala, Spain.

36. Accidental omission in the calendar of OBk, supplied for by a later hand; the corresponding formula is in the original hand, f. 169v.

37. The scribe of the OBk calendar has carelessly omitted St Bartholomew, and re-placed him by the double entry which belongs to the following day. The proper sequence is found in the OBk itself, f. 176r, and in PO, ff. 90v-91r.

38. In Cistercian calendars after 1147, the order of entries varies: Giles sometimes comes first, since only he rates a conventual Mass, but sometimes Priscus comes first, since a martyr takes precedence over a simple confessor. The Paraclete scribe responsible for the model which lies behind the calendar of OBk, copied the two Cistercian entries, raising the first--Giles-- to Twelve Lesson rank. He then added St Loup after the commemoration entry, also giving St Loup a Twelve Lesson rank! The proper entry should have read: *Egidii et Lupi confessorum XII.*

Prisci martyris com--and this is what we find indicated in OBk,
ff. 177v-180r; and in PO 93r-93v.

39.   The Paraclete calendar and the corresponding entries in OBk and
PO add *sociorumque eius* to St Adrian's name.

40.   Omitted by first hand, and supplied by a much later one. That
this was simply yet another oversight of the original scribe is
shown by PO, ff. 100v-101r, and f. 120v. The collect is given
in OBk, f. 186r, with an implicit reference to the Common for
rest of the Office.

41.   The Paraclete scribe has once again forgotten to indicate the
rank of celebration, which is that of Twelve Lessons. See OBk,
f. 189r; and PO, f. 102r and f. 120v. There is something Freud-
ian about this *lapsus calami:* at the Paraclete, the reduction
of Jerome to anything less than a Twelve Lesson feast would
have been as serious as celebrating Christmas under the rite
of a simple commemoration!

42.   Only here has the Paraclete calendar really corrected a Cistercian anomaly, since it is probably the same Germanus mentioned here, who also appears earlier, under the date of July
31.   On the other hand, in spite of the Paraclete distinction
between Rémy, with his Twelve Lessons, and Vasst and Amandus
with their joint commemoration, OBk, ff. 189r-189v, and PO,
ff. 102r-102v, combine all three confessors in a single Twelve
Lesson formulary; while PO, f. 120v, indicates that Vaast and
Amandus receive Twelve Lesson honors.

43.   The concurrence of the anniversary of the Dedication of the
Paraclete with the Feast of St Denis and Companions has resul-
ted in the transfer of the latter to the following day.

44.   Not explicitly mentioned in many Cistercian calendars, and in
none from an early period; but this celebration is described
in the earliest redaction of the Order's customary. See the
Chapter, 'De Officiis defunctorum precipuis'--edited in the
earliest known version by Fr Bruno Griesser, *Die* Ecclesiastica
Officia Cisterciensis Ordinis *des Cod. 1711 von Trient,* in ASOC
12 (1956) 216-17.

45.   Given only a commemoration in the calendar, which is surprising
in this aggressively feminist nunnery. But Homer has been nod-
ding, as is proved by a glance at OBk, f. 204 v, and PO, f. 113v.

46. Wrongly entered as Euphemia in the calendar, but easily corrected by the corresponding rubrics in OBk and PO. Eugenia enjoyed a special *cultus* at the Paraclete, Christmas notwithstanding. Abelard makes special mention of her at the very end of his *Letter 7, On the Origin of Nuns*, PL 178:256 C; or, in the edition by J. T. Muckle, *Medieval Studies* 17 (1955) 281. Among Eugenia's special titles to veneration by the Paraclete community was the fact that, having lived in disguise as a monk for a number of years, she was finally elected *abbot* by her unsuspecting confrères. She made a fine abbot.

47. See pp. 44-60 of the book referred to above, note 22.

48. Jean Deshusses, *Le Sacramentaire grégorien: Ses principales formes d'après les plus anciens manuscrits (Spicilegium Friburgense*, 16; Fribourg [Suisse], 1971).

49. OBk, f. 153v.

50. *Op. S. Bern.*, 3:515: 'Inter cetera quae optime aemulati sunt patres nostri, Cisterciensis videlicet ordinis inchoatores, hoc quoque studiosissime et religiosissime curaverunt, ut in divinis laudibus id canerent quod magis *authenticum* inveniretur.' (ET *Prologue to the Cistercian Antiphonary*, CF 1:161).

51. For a brief discussion and bibliography of material relating to St Gregory's role as a composer of liturgical chant, see Chrysogonus Waddell, 'The Origin and Early Evolution of the Cistercian Antiphonary: Reflections on Two Cistercian Chant Reforms,' in M. Basil Pennington (ed.), *The Cistercian Spirit: A Symposium in Honor of Thomas Merton.* CFS 3, pp. 196-197, footnote 11.

52. *Vita Gregorii Magni*, in PL 75:91.

53. *Prologus*, p. 515: 'Tandem aliquando, non sustinentibus iam fratribus nostris abbatibus ordinis, cum mutari et corrigi placuisset, curae nostrae id operis iniunxerunt.' (ET *Prologue*, CF 1:161.)

54. Waddell, 'Origin,' pp. 209-218.

55. For a brief treatment of this type of 'chant dialect' as an offshoot of gregorian chant, see Paul H. Lang, *Music in Western Civilization* (New York, 1941) pp. 71-72.

56. *Ibid.*, p. 71.

57. *Prefatio seu tractatus de cantu seu correctione antiphonarii*,
     PL 182:1132 A: '...quod nostrum ab aliis ratio fecit diversum.'

58. *Prologus*, p. 515: '...de multis et diversis novum tandem anti-
     phonarium in subiectum volumen collegimus....' (ET *Prologue*,
     CF 1:161-162.)

59. Edited integrally for the first time by Jean Leclercq, *Pierre
     le Vénérable* (Abbaye S. Wandrille, 1946) pp. 379-90.

60. *Letter 10*, PL 178:339 D-340 A: 'Diebus Dominicae sepulturae
     antiquam consuetudinem penitus abstulistis. Ubi et invitatori-
     um et hymnum cum tribus tantum lectionibus et responsoriis cum
     Gloria contra omnem Ecclesiae morem, et, ut dicitur, rationem
     vos dicere instituistis.' (Punctuation at the beginning of
     the text altered in keeping with the meaning of the text, which
     apparently escaped the editor.)

61. RB, c. 15: 'A Pentecoste autem usque caput Quadragesimae omni-
     bus noctibus cum sex posterioribus psalmis tantum ad Nocturnos
     dicatur [*Alleluia*]. Omni vero Dominica extra Quadragesimam
     Cantica, Matutini, Prima, Tertia, Sexta, Nonaque cum *Alleluia*
     dicantur.'

62. In the Hanslick edition, CSEL 75: Cap. 9, 4: 'Inde sequatur
     ambrosianum'; cap. 12, 4: '...responsorium, ambrosianum, versu
     ...'; cap. 13, 11: '...responsorium, ambrosianum, versu...';
     cap. 17, 8: '...responsorium, ambrosianum, versu....'

63. Smaragdus, in his *Commentaria in Regulam Sancti Benedicti*,
     writes, when treating of Ch. 9, PL 102:834: 'Inde sequatur
     Ambrosianus. Id est hymnus. Ambrosianum dicit, vel divinum,
     vel coeleste, id est divinitus, vel coelitus inspiratum.
     Alii Ambrosianum ab Ambrosio hymnorum magistro dici volunt.'
     Smaragdus simply follows in the line of Hildemar and Paul the
     Deacon. See Pauli Warnefridi, *In Sanctam Regulam Commentarium*
     (Typis Abbatiae Montis Casini, 1880) p. 232.

64. *Letter 10*, PL 178:339 BD: '...Hymnos solitos respuistis, et
     quosdam apud nos inauditos, et fere omnibus Ecclesiis incog-
     nitos, ac minus sufficientes, introduxistis. Unde et per totum
     annum in vigiliis tam feriarum quam festivitatum uno hymno et
     eodem contenti estis [Abelard is referring to *Aeterne rerum
     conditor*]....'

65. Troyes, Bibliothèque municipale, MS 1467, ff. 33r-37r.

66. See Bruno Stäblein, *Monumenta Monodica Medii Aevi* 1: *Hymnen* (I) (Kassel, Basel, 1956), where, in his notes commenting on the Cistercian hymn repertory, pp. 515-22, he makes out a case for Cistercian authorship of the hymns transcribed in the section, 'Zisterzienser Hymnar,' pp. 26-83, and numbered, according to his numerical identification of specific hymn melodies, 57 *Magnum salutis gaudium*, 58 *Ad cenam agni providi*, 59[1] *Chorus novae Jerusalem*, 60 *Optatus votis omnium*, 61 *Jesu, nostra redemptio*, 63 *Jam Christus astra ascenderat*, 65[1] *Stephano primo martyri*, 66 *Mysterium Ecclesiae*, 69[1] *Almi prophetae*, and 70[1] *Sanctorum meritis*.

67. *Magnum salutis gaudium*, *Optatus votis omnium*, *Iam Christus astra ascenderat*, *Mysterium Ecclesiae*, *Almi prophetae*, *Iesu nostra redemptio*, *Ad cenam Agni providi*, and *O quam glorifica* --though I have some doubts about the last two melodies. Stablein's commentary needs careful control, and his transcriptions are not always entirely accurate.

68. Twice edited by G. M. Dreves: first, with the title *Petri Abaelardi Peripatetici Palantini Hymnarius Paraclitensis, sive Hymnorum libri tres* (Paris, 1891), and later in *Analecta Hymnica* 48 (Leipzig, 1905) pp. 141-232. These editions have superseded the defective version edited by Dom Pitra, in PL 178:1765-1816, and the still more defective edition in Victor Cousin, *Petri Abaelardi opera hactenus seorsim edita* (Paris, 1849) I, 295ff. The eagerly awaited new edition by the noted hymnologist, Josef Szövérffy, should be in print by the spring or summer of 1975.

69. AH 48, pp. 142-144; PL 178:1771-74.

70. AH 48, p. 143; PL 178:1771.

71. AH 48, ppl 143-144; PL 178:1771-74.

72. AH 48, p. 191; PL 178:1803.

73. Peter became abbot of Saint-Gildas sometime around 1125; scholarly opinion is divided as to the exact year in which he washed his hands, once for all, of the irreformable community. This might have been as late as 1135, but as early as 1132. One of our best authorities on Abelard's theology, Fr E. Buytaert, writes in his introduction to *Petri Abaelardi Opera Theologica* 1. CC. *Continuatio Mediaevalis* 11, p. X: 'The situation became so desperate [at Saint-Gildas] that around 1132 Abelard fled the place. Between 1132 and 1135-36 he seems to have wandered

around considerably, staying frequently at the Paraclete, until
he decided to settle again in Paris and start teaching and writing theology (not later than 1136).'

74. *Epistola consolatoria;* translation taken from J. T. Muckle,
The Story of Abelard's Adversities (Toronto, Canada, 1954)
p. 61.

75. Orderic Vital, *Historia ecclesiastica* 3, VIII, 25, in PL 188:
641 C: 'Aditus suos satis obserant, et secreta summopere celant.
Nullum alterius ecclesiae monachum in suis penetralibus admit-
tunt, nec in oratorium ad missam vel alia servitia secum ingre-
di permittunt.'

76. *Epistola consolatoria,* Muckle translation, p. 61.

77. PL 178:677-730.

78. PL 178:729-84.

79. In the paper, 'Fraud, Fiction, and Borrowing in the Correspondence of Abelard and Heloise,' presented at the *Colloque international Pierre Abélard-Pierre le Vénérable* held at Cluny in
July, 1972, to be published in the *Actes* of the colloquium.

80. The monograph by Stephanus Hilpisch, *Die Doppelklöster: Ent-
stehung und Organisation (Beiträge zur Geschichte des alten
Mönchtums und des Benediktinerordens* 15; Münster/Westfalen,
1928), needs to be brought up to date, but still remains a
good general introduction to the study of double-monasteries.

81. Edited by T. P. McLaughlin, 'Abelard's Rule for Religious
Women,' in *Mediaeval Studies* 18 (1956) 241-92. This edition
supercedes the version in PL 178:255-326.

82. A detailed description of the nunnery of Coyroux, served by
the monks of Obazine, is given in Lib. II, cap. 1 of *Vita
beati Stephani abbatis monasterii Obazinensis.* For the editions, see note 10, above.

83. April 21, 1142, is the generally accepted date, even though
the contemporary sources are generally on the vague side. See
E. Buytaert, p. XII of the General Introduction referred to
above, note 73. Fr Buytaert personally opts for the year 1144.

84. The papal privilege issued for the Paraclete by Hadrian IV,
from the Lateran Palace, and under the date December 1, 1157,

lists the entire series of Paraclete foundations. See the text in PL 188:1529 CD, with further references to other editions in Jaffé, *Regesta* 2, p. 127, n. 10313 (6996). GCh 7 and 12, in the entries devoted to the Paraclete and the Paraclete foundations, are somewhat unreliable.

85. Almost all these communities were transferred elsewhere during the upheavals of the seventeenth century, with the consequent loss of much that was associated with them in the early years of their existence. Still, it might be well worth the effort to try to track down whatever *liturgica* of these nunneries might still be extant from the early days, since such material might help throw further light on life at the Paraclete.

86. The *incipit* given in the version in PL 178:313–17, which follows the *editio princeps*, is incorrect. Read *Institutiones nostrae* for *Instructiones nostrae*. D. Van den Eynde drew attention to this important Paraclete document, by his article, 'En marge des écrits d'Abélard: Les *Excerpta ex regulis Paracletensis monasterii*,' in *Analecta Praemonstratensia* 38 (1962) 70–84. A number of the mysteries attached to *Institutiones nostrae* were cleared up by John Benton, in his article, 'The Paraclete and the Council of Rouen of 1231,' in the *Bulletin of Medieval Canon Law*, n.s. 4 (1974).

87. PL 178:313 D.

88. Lalore, *Cartulaire*, p. 72.

89. *Libellus II, Praefatio*, AH 48, p. 164; PL 178:1787: 'Quos [hymnos] ita compositos esse cognoscatis, ut bipartitus sit eorum cantus sicut et rhythmus, et sit una omnibus nocturnis melodia communis atque altera diurnis sicut et rhythmus.'

90. See Bruno Stäblein, *Hymnen (I)*, 514, where the author's description of the 'modern' Cistercian melodies of the Bernardine reform is used by Lorenz Weinrich to describe the characteristics of the melody of Abelard's *O quanta qualia:* 'Peter Abaelard as Musician--I,' *The Musical Quarterly* 55 (1969) 304. Unfortunately, the author's notes on the Cistercian hymnal are highly inaccurate.

ST BERNARD AND THE PAGAN CLASSICS:
AN HISTORICAL VIEW

THOMAS RENNA

Was there a monastic attitude towards pagan literature during
the early Middle Ages? While historians prior to the 1920s stressed the monks' hostility toward the latin classics, more recent scholarship refers to monastic humanism, that is, the monks' tendency to
admire and even to assimilate the style and content of antique works.
At the least, many monks read the classics as a preparation for divine studies. But what about the persistent minority of monks who
condemned the study of the classics? Historians usually reply that
the two traditions simply co-existed, with the hostile view assum-
ing perhaps a quasi-official status--at least after the eighth century.

But rather than speak of two traditions toward the classics--
as if one excluded the other--it would be more useful to adopt the
categories absolute and relative. Just as Augustine contrasted the
earthly and heavenly manifestations of the *civitas Dei*, so too the
monks displayed a dual attitude towards non-christian literature.
In the light of eternity letters are as nothing. But as an aid to
salvation (e.g., as a linguistic tool for the study of Scripture)
the *trivium* possesses relative value.

But which of these two attitudes towards the classics can properly be termed monastic? While the monastic outlook which opposed
liberal study might be more consistent with ascetic renunciation, it
probably never reflected the prevailing view in early medieval monasteries. Monks utilized the ancient writings in much the same way as
did clerics. Certainly no literary argument either for or against
classical study was a monopoly of the monks. It may be premature to
speak of a bona fide monastic attitude towards pagan literature--at
least before the eleventh century. The Cistercians of the early
twelfth century best illustrate the character of this more formal
attitude. While the various elements of this view had been present
since the later Roman Empire, they were not crystallized into anything like a theory until the monastic revival of 1050-1150.

Insofar as western monks were concerned, the solutions of Origen, Ambrose, Jerome, and Augustine had the greatest influence on
the monastic literary posture towards learning. Medieval monks often echo the patristic suspicion of pagan doctrines, idolatries,
and obscenities. But most influential was the association of pagan
works with the world, an idea expanded by Pope Gregory the Great.[1]
Ancient letters came to be seen more as secular than as pagan as
germanic Europe moved away from its roman roots. Irish and anglo-

saxon monks did not feel threatened by a remote roman past.

All this does not add up to a consistent monastic perception of the classics. Benedict[2] and Cassiodorus[3] approved of the study of literature, while Cassian[4] and Isidore[5] did not. The tradition was established that since the pagan classics were dangerous, they had to be treated solely as a *means* to higher ends: their use had to be justified in terms of the goals of the ascetic life. Often in an *accessus* an author would mention one of the standard patristic images (Israelites stealing gold from Egypt, or taking Canaanite wives) without further comment. All of the clichés summoned by monks are repeated in clerical writings.[6]

The carolingian monastic reforms compelled monks to continue rationalizing their handling of classical texts. In the ninth and tenth centuries defenders of the classics professed to see in them much wisdom. Even the beauty of the literary images can inspire the christian reader to nobler thoughts. On the other side, the critics of classical study stress the risks secular study brings to the quest for God.[7] Sensual delight in the use of language and literary images can ensnare the holy soul in base things. No doubt the further elaboration of monastic theology helped to clarify the monk's perspective of the *auctores*. For some monks it was becoming evident that extraneous learning made no contribution to the soul's ascent to union with God in the silence of the cloister. The majority of monks who read and utilized the classics felt no such qualms.[8]

In the eleventh century the rise of clerical schools and a monastic resurgence provided the conditions proper for the appearance of a more distinctly monastic notion of education. The monks needed a philosophy which would separate them from the cathedral schools and would suit their isolated life. Monks attacked classical learning as incompatible with their own unique objectives. These criticisms --formerly made almost casually in a variety of contexts[9]--appear within formal defenses of the monastic way. In his treatise on monks Peter Damian excluded the unnecessary parts of monastic training.[10] Liberal studies are trivial because they did nothing to the holy soul's search for God in the fire of love. Whereas a tenth-century monastic critic of the classics might repeat one of the standard arguments against them, Damian incorporates his critique within a treatise on the perfection of monks. Instead of replying to the usual retort that liberal studies are necessary to train the monk for scriptural studies, Damian prefers to render the argument irrelevant. Liberal learning is unrelated to the monk's weeping, and is therefore superfluous. He does not see the classics as particularly dangerous or immoral. Since the focus of monastic life is interior peace, anything which disturbs this quiet is to be omitted. Even the reading of the Scripture is in this sense secondary to the monk's inner life. No doubt many reformers, like Damian, were repelled by the fame and

influence of well-known monastic schools such as Bec. Extrabibli-
cal studies reminded them of the noise and bustle of these not-so-
cloistered monastic learning centers, as well as the dynamic cathedral schools.

Damian's emphasis on the need for a monk formerly trained in
liberal studies to convert to the *schola Christi* was in fact a common motif in eleventh and twelfth-century writing. When a school-
master entered Cluny he converted to humility.[11] David of Himmerod
abandoned his studies to be instructed in the Rule of Benedict.[12]
Peter of Celle,[13] Peter Comestor,[14] and Rupert of Deutz[15] voice similar sentiments.

This notion of conversion from liberal studies to monastic *phi-
losophia* is linked to the tradition which associated classical with
worldly values. In semi-autobiographical passages, monastic writers
of the ninth and tenth centuries often express reservations about
their pursuit of non-christian works.[16] Some even abandoned such
studies late in life, as in the archetypical instance of Alcuin.
But these inner struggles should not be taken too literally, for
they are often only rhetorical flourishes, well established by tradition, which added heroic stature to an author (did not Jerome and
Augustine suffer the same anguish?). Such self-revelations signaled
an acute moral sense, and could excuse continued study of the suspicious writings. Also, a monk-reader would be warned not to become
inordinately attached to secular things. These literary expressions
of spiritual turmoil show that monks had not yet discovered a con-
vincing way to assimilate antique literature with their own work of
copying, examining, and absorbing these texts.

But the conversions from liberal studies to the *schola Christi*
between 1050-1150 have a note of personal commitment. The emphasis
is now more on the change from one *ordo* in the church to another,
and less on the change of the subjects being studied. As the contemplative life became more clearly defined, so too did the monastic
attitude towards the classics. It is misleading to call the new
monks anti-humanists[17] as if they were simply resisting a pedagogi-
cal trend. It would be more accurate to think of the distrust of
the traditional *trivium* as resulting from a reassessment of the direction of monastic life. Also, the closing of external schools
was partially the outcome of the popularity of the cathedral centers.
In their opposition to the classics the new monks were not so much
against something, as *for* the purity of the cloister. They were concerned with that which a monk was converted *to*, not what he was converted from. This tendency to evaluate secular study in terms of a
monk's spiritual needs can be seen most clearly in Bernard of Clairvaux.

As an abstract issue, the merits of the liberal arts held no
interest for Bernard. His approach was practical: did the classics

contribute to the monk's spiritual progress? His answer was a re-
sounding no. The liberal disciplines failed Bernard's twofold test
for the types of knowledge suitable for monks.

First, the *artes liberales* do not increase a monk's love, self-
knowledge, or humility.[18] The monk is concerned only with *scientia*
which pertains directly to his salvation. Since secular letters do
not make a monk weep, they are superfluous. It is impossible for a
monk to make progress if he lacks humility. But humility derives
from self-knowledge which comes from the personal experience of sol-
itary prayer. Since secular knowledge detracts from such experience,
it can only lead to pride--the major obstacle to self-knowledge. Indeed, liberal *scientia* can be dangerous for a monk since it cannot
be put to practical use, that is, the service of others. The acquis-
ition of secular learning can be justified only if it is utilized in
the refutation of error and the instruction of Christians. But since
the monk's task is to save himself, such knowledge would become a
burden and, so to speak, a sin.[19] It would be bottled up inside a
monk's heart with no outlet, resulting in an arrogant attempt to a-
bandon his proper duties.

Second, the liberal arts are incompatible with the monk's peculiar ways of knowing God. The kinds of *scientia* proper for a monk
are knowledge of self and of God.[20] All other types of *scientia*
simply distract the monk from these primary goals; they may destroy
the basis of monastic life. Bernard goes so far as to imply that
monks lack the virtue necessary to undertake such a chance. Only
the strong, the clerics, should dare to assume so perilous a ven-
ture.[21] His subordination of monks to clerics (those who do study
the classics) is partially ironic, for the monk is warned not to
deem himself superior to others. Above all he must not rank himself above prelates, who are called to administer the church. While
monks may be higher than clerics in the charismatic hierarchy they
are lower than clerics in the normal operation of the institutional
ecclesia--a recurring motif in Bernard's writings.[22] This reproof
of the monks' improper desire for what is forbidden is also a rhetorical device aimed at clarifying the characteristics--especially
the humility--of the monastic way. Bernard never misses an oppor-
tunity to contrast the spiritualities of clerics and monks. Typical also is Bernard's castigation of monks who hanker to become prelates.

Throughout his discussion of monastic knowledge Bernard explains why the study of the *auctores* is permitted and even necessary for clerics.[23] Here Bernard repeats the usual arguments in
favor of grammar and rhetoric as aids to the study of Scripture,
the refutation of heretics and schismatics, and the instruction of
the faithful. He also implies that liberal study increases a prelate's effectiveness as an administrator and defender of the church's

customs and rights. Bernard is more original, however, when he
stresses the contribution of letters to the cleric's peacemaking
activities, and the connection between active charity and learning.[24] Bernard's distinction between clerical learning as service
and monastic learning as personal/experiential is, in fact, an
element of his ecclesiology. Whereas Peter Damian merely hinted
at the ecclesiological dimensions of monastic knowledge, Bernard
incorporated his critique of secular letters into a comprehensive
ecclesiology and monastic theology.

Bernard's emphasis on the different modes of knowing makes it
unnecessary for him to respond to the two conventional justifica-
tions for profane learning—usefulness as a preparation for divine
studies, and as an inducement to the practice of ascetic virtue.
By focusing on the essential principles of monastic spirituality,
Bernard does not feel compelled to elaborate on the linguistic
skills needed to handle biblical texts. Apparently he believed
that only a minimum of facility in Latin—acquired without resort
to classical aids—was sufficient for cloistered monks.[25]

Bernard saw no merit in the view that the classics provided
edifying models of ascetic behavior.[26] He clearly wanted to cut
away the intellectual base of this argument, common at the time.
Since the monastic revival of the eleventh century the appeal to
pagan authors for support of monastic conduct was gaining acceptance among monks. The idea that the classics contain moral wisdom
dates back to the Fathers, and was firmly established by the ninth
century. It was very much alive in the twelfth century when many
authors, such as John of Salisbury, exhorted readers to the natural
virtue found in the classics.[27] Those monks who strove to retain
classical study in the internal schools tried to justify its use
in terms of monastic ends. Conrad of Hirsau[28] and William of Saint-
Denis[29] would have the ancient poets and philosophers teach us contemplation, discipline of the flesh, and contempt of the world.
But Bernard no doubt thought it ridiculous that Aeneas' wanderings
could show a monk how to be detached. Why go to pagan sources to
find quasi-models of ascetic virtue when more genuine ideals could
be found in Scripture? At any rate, Bernard would have his monks
learn about God in the silence of their cells; literary paradigms
have little to do with the *schola Christi*.

Traditionally monastic writers stressed the need for a pure
motive when approaching the classics, lest the unwary be seduced
by the errors, sensual delight, and blasphemies contained in them.
They imply that only monks possessed the virtue to enable them to
ward off such temptations. Bernard, however, shifts the prerequi-
site for high motive to *clerics*, not monks. This surprise reversal
of motives is an effective rhetorical technique, for it summons
both clerics and monks to the elevated moral ideals proper to their

own calling. The cleric must build and maintain a solid ascetic base before attempting to study the *auctores* and put them to practical use. The monk must rise to a level of humility which will allow him to rest in the Holy Spirit. Thus in his very denial of secular studies for contemplatives Bernard outlines a sublime doctrine of monastic *scientia*.

When Bernard's letters to schoolmasters and ecclesiastics concerning worldly learning[30] are considered in the context of this epistemology, it becomes clear that Bernard opposed the study of pagan writings not as such, but only for monks. Bernard took it for granted that clerics, especially bishops, pursue the liberal arts in their preparation for pastoral work. He employs rhetorical exaggeration in his blasts against the ancient authors--which he himself cites often[31]--in order to point to their function as a *means* to an end (the practice of active charity). What is important is that clerics possess sufficient virtue before they study, and they utilize their knowledge for the ends appropriate to their vocation. Malachy's teacher was light-headed[32] not because the works he read were bad in themselves, but because he lacked the preparatory virtue and the knowledge of what to do with this learning once he had acquired it. The more clear-sighted Malachy, already converted to God, puts this knowledge to good use for the rest of his episcopal career.[33] In accordance with many monastic writers of the early twelfth century Bernard treats ancient letters not as pagan or evil, but as worldly--to be exploited as one would any other creature.

CONCLUSIONS

1. The tendency among twelfth-century monastic writers was to limit classical studies to *clerics*. In the patristic age there were numerous ecclesiastical prohibitions against both monks and clerics engaging in liberal pursuits. The uneasy compromise between the hostile and favorable view of the classics was resolved in terms of function. The emphasis in the twelfth century was less upon the dangers inherent in pagan writings, and more upon the state of life appropriate to specific types of learning. The purpose of the *ordo* and its respective epistemological methods determined its course of study. Liberal studies were placed firmly within a broader ecclesiological context.

2. Bernard's critique of the pagan classics illustrates the growing separation of the ascetic and liberal arts traditions. In a sense, the traditional monastic tirades against liberal learning demonstrate the close ties monastic spirituality had with Latin literature. But in the twelfth century the monks had less use for this relationship as they formulated an elaborate theology based

on Scripture and personal ascetic experience. The decline of the
classics in monastic education--and the diminishing influence of
monastic education in general--is one part of a european-wide movement in education. But this development was not a case of sour
grapes, that is, the monks rejecting what was forbidden. Rather,
it reveals the maturation of monastic theology, now less dependent
on non-monastic sources. No longer did monks need fear the re-
proach: Thou art not a monk. Thou art a Ciceronean.

NOTES

1. PL 75:42, 516, 947, 972; PL 76:72–92; PL 79:355f. See C. Dagens, *Saint Grégoire le Grand* (Paris, 1977) 31–54.

2. See J. Leclercq, *The Love of Learning and the Desire for God,* translated C. Misrahi (New York, 1974) 13–24.

3. *Variarum* 9:21 (MGH, *Auctores antiq.* 12:286).

4. *De coenobiorum instit. lib. 5*; PL 49:250, 979.

5. *Sententiarum Lib. 3*; PL 83:685, 877.

6. Cf. Rhabanus Maurus, *De clericorum institutione* (PL 107:395–98, 404f.),Hildebert, *Epistola* 1 (PL 171:141f.), Honorius of Autun, *Speculum ecclesiae* (PL 172:1056). As do many authors between 800–1200, Honorius condemns the classics with equal vehemence (*Spec. ecclesiae;* PL 172:1085).

7. Arnold of St. Emmeram, *Ad provisorem Sancti Emmerammi;* MGH, *Scriptores* 4:546 and Hugh Metel in R. Ceillier, *Histoire générale des auteurs sacrés* 14 (1858) 367.

8. See J. Leclercq, 'L'humanisme bénédictin du VIIIe au XIIe siècle,' *Analecta monastica* (Rome, 1948) 1–20, and 'L'humanisme des moines au moyen âge,' *A. Ermini* (Spoleto, 1970) 69–113; A. Wilmart, 'Une riposte de l'ancien monachisme au manifeste de Saint Bernard,' *Revue bénédictine* 46 (1934) 296–344; J. P. Bonnes, 'Une lettre du Xe siècle,' *Revue Mabillon* 33 (1943) 23–47.

9. E.g., d'Achery, ed., *Spicilegium* (Paris, 1723) 2:77, 338, 392; *Thietmari,* MGH, *Scriptores* 3:748; *Vita Popponis,* MGH, *SS* 11:314.

10. *De perfectione monachorum;* PL 145:306f.; cf. 232, 560, 695, 699, 831. Cf. Gauthier, *Liber contra 4 labyrinthos;* PL 199:1145, Rupert, *De omnipotentia Dei;* PL 170:473.

11. Cf. Peter the Venerable, *Epistola* 3; PL 189:279, and Roscelin to Abelard, *Epistola* 15; PL 178:370D.

12. *Vita B. Davidis,* ed. A. Schneider; *Analecta S. Ord. Cist.* (1955) 33.

13. *Epistola* 73; PL 202:519.

14. Sermo 9; PL 198:1747, 1822. Cf. Bernard, SC 30.10; SBOp 1:219; CF 7:121.

15. *In Regula S. Ben.* 1; PL 170:480.

16. Cf. Othlo of St Emmeram, *De tentationibus suis;* PL 146:29-58, *Liber visionum,* 353-57.

17. G. Paré, A. Brunet, P. Tremblay, *La Renaissance du XIIe siècle: Les écoles et l'enseignement* (Ottawa, 1933) 180-90. Cf. P. Delhaye, 'L'Organisation scolaire au XIIe siècle,' *Traditio* 5 (1947) 211-68 at 225-34.

18. Bernard, SC 36:2-7, 37:5-7; SBOp 2:4-8, 11-14; CF 7:174-86.

19. SC 36:4; SBOp 2:6; CF 7:176-77. The monk's knowledge of himself and God is *scientia,* here synonymous with *cognitio* and *notitia.*

20. SC 37:2-7, 38:2-5; SBOp 2:9-14; CF 7:182-91. In another sense, knowledge is only the preparation for the possession or experience of God (SC 23:14; SBOp 1:147; CF 7:37f.).

21. SC 23:6-7, 14; SBOp 1:141-43, 147-48; CF 7:30-31, 37-38; SC 36:2-3, 37:2; SBOp 2:4-6, 9-10; CF 7:174-76, 182.

22. Cf. SC 46; SBOp 2:56-61; CF 7:241-47.

23. SC 36:1-3, 37:2; SBOp 2:4-5, 9; CF 7:173-76, 182. See J. Sommerfeldt, 'Epistemology, Education and Social Theory in the Thought of Bernard of Clairvaux,' *Saint Bernard of Clairvaux,* CS 28 (Kalamazoo, 1977) 169-79.

24. Cf. SC 12:1, 3, 5, 9-11; SBOp 1:60-67; CF 4:76-82, 84-86; *Ad clericos de conversione;* SBOp 4:106-16.

25. See notes 18-20 above.

26. I draw this conclusion from Bernard's neglect of classical learning in his treatments of proper monastic endeavors (e.g., SC 36-37 on knowledge). Even when he lists reasons why prelates should pursue letters (above, notes 23, 24) he never mentions possible benefits for ascetic practice. Cf. *Epistola* 42; SBOp 7:100-31.

27. *Metalogicus;* PL 199:853-56, *passim.*

28. R. Huygens, ed., *Conrad de Hirsau: Dialogues super auctores* (Brussels, 1955) 47-60, *passim*. Cf. Anselm, *Epistola* 55; PL 158:1124f.

29. A. Wilmart, ed., 'Une dialogue apologétique du moine Guillaume, biographe de Suger,' *Revue Mabillon* 32 (1942) 82-118. Cf. Peter of Blois, *Epistola* 101; PL 207:311f.

30. See *Epistolae* 104, 108 (SBOp 7:261-63, 277-79); 250, 523 (SBOp 8:145-47, 486-89). Cf. *In soll Petri et Pauli* 1:3 (SBOp 5: 189f.); *In die Pentec.* 3:5 (SBOp 5:173f.).

31. See B. Jacqueline, 'Répertoire des citations d'auteurs profanes,' *Bernard de Clairvaux* (Paris, 1953) 549-54, and E. Franceschini's review in *Aevum* 28 (1954) 571-73. Bernard employs rhetorical techniques with ease. See E. Kennan, 'Rhetoric and Style in the *De consideratione*,' *Studies in Medieval Cistercian History*, II, CS 24 (Kalamazoo, 1976) 40-48. Clearly Bernard did not consider himself always bound by the rules he proposed for his monks. He saw himself as a reformer of monastic and clerical discipline, with the prerogative to intervene in emergencies. For Bernard as outsider and prophet, see T. Renna, 'Abelard versus Bernard: An Event in Monastic History,' *Cîteaux* 27 (1976) 189-202.

32. Malachy observed his teacher tearing up his walls: *Et solo visu offensus puer serius, quod levitatem redoleret, resilivit ab eo, ac deinceps illum nec videre curavit. Ita cum esset studiosissimus litterarum prae honesto tamen sprevit eas virtutis amator* (*Vita Malachiae* 2; SBOp 3:311; CF 10:17). Cf. Bernard's rhetorical use of no knowledge of letters (SC 26:7).

33. *Vita Malachiae;* SBOp 3:314-17, 325f., 339f., etc.; CF 10:21-25, 33, 48.

THE APPEAL TO REASON IN ST BERNARD'S
DE DILIGENDO DEO (II:2-6)

LUKE ANDERSON, O. CIST.

'But if unbelievers blind themselves to these truths--namely
that [1] the *reason* for loving God is God himself and [2] that the
way to love God is to love him beyond measure--God is still ready
to confound their ingratitude with his numberless benefits conferred for man's advantage and manifest to human sense.'[1]

This is St Bernard's topic sentence and it contains the truths
he will defend and the defense by which he will validate these
truths. God manifests his *in se* loveableness--'the cause of loving...is God.' And the manifestation requires a response that is
measureless--'the way is to love Him beyond measure.'[2] These are
the truths which reason alone can divine. But reason will not per-
ceive the validity of these truths without argumentation.

God's gifts manifest his loveableness. And since they are
conferred for man's advantage, man can begin his response at a
minimum level in the context of an ordered self-love and climb to
maximum love when he perceives the absolute and *in se* good. But
the benefits and their conferral for man's advantage are manifest
to human reason whether that human mind is simply without faith or
positively inimical to it. Thus we must make an analysis of three
phrases: the innumerable gifts. their conferral on man; and their
manifestation to human sense.[3]

1. *Man's Benefits*

St Bernard treats of two kinds of human goods. He begins with
those things which benefit man's body: bread, sun and air. These
he denominates as *the more necessary goods* since they pertain to
the body as it is the substratum of the soul's life.[4] St Bernard
turns abruptly to consider another constellation of goods, *the
higher goods;* these goods reside in that permanent part of man, his
soul.[5] Bernard defines these goods and compares them. He first
defines man's *dignity* in terms of man's free will which makes him
at once free in himself and superior to, and the ruler of, others.[6]
He then defines man's *knowledge* as that by which he recognizes his
dignity as inherent but its source as extrinsic.[7] Lastly, he defines *virtue* as that by which man ardently seeks God from whom he
has his being and valiantly holds him when he is found.[8] Free will
gives man a power, but knowledge recognizes that what is given is
indeed given by another; and virtue seeks the face of the *giver*.
The goods reveal something beyond themselves.

Then Bernard compares these *bona ementiora*: dignity is not
knowledge, nor are dignity and knowledge virtue; and virtue is neither knowledge nor dignity. Each is a good. Each is a distinct
good. Hence they are limited, diverse, and in the light of comparisons gradational. So, for example, unrecognized freedom is of
no avail; it may prove harmful. Again, fragmentary knowledge may
issue in a false judgement about man's dignity. And again, a knowledge of man's worth must necessarily include a knowledge of its
origin, for a thing is not known without its cause being dimly ap-
prehended. And finally, virtue will be authentic when it prevents
man from arrogating to himself a good, the glory of which belongs
to another--God; and *a fortiori* such virtue prevents the destruc-
tion of the glory of God by pursuing the God from whom the good derives its reality.[9] And hence St Bernard can say:

> It is evident, there, that *dignity* is altogether useless
> without *knowledge*, and *knowledge* without *virtue* sinful.
> But the man of virtue to whom neither knowledge can be
> sinful nor dignity unfruitful, lifts up his voice to
> God and frankly confesses: 'Not to us, O Lord, not to
> us: but to your name give glory.'[10]

Thus, St Bernard views bread, sun and air as specific goods, specific perfections and specific and indeed univocal in meaning. They
are gifts of God, but do not image him.

Initially, the same can be said of man's triple, more eminent
goods. Dignity, knowledge, and virtue, are specific goods, by
definition, specific perfections, and specific and indeed univocal
in meaning. But when St Bernard compares these goods he moves into another realm. Now man's spiritual goods are seen as perfections
of another order. They are *simple perfections*--by nature transcendental. They are diverse, limited and gradational, and by extension
participated. in contradistinction to man's material goods, these
spiritual goods are deficient but authentic similitudes of a higher
good. Man's spiritual goods are images of God. Word usage here is
analogous.

The *a posteriori* argument, drawn from the *de facto* existence
of simple perfections, which sees man's spiritual goods as redolent
of God's goods, furnishes St Bernard with the fundamental appeal to
reason. Thus there is truth *in* man, but in the last analysis this
predication can only be made in the virtue of another fact: 'For
the Lord *is* truth.'[11] Clearly we find overtones here of the celebrated *Quarta Via*, and the *id quod maxime est* thesis. In an apos-
trophe full of metaphysical overtones St Bernard says: '...We attribute to ourselves, O Lord, neither any knowledge nor any dignity;
but to your name from whom all proceeds do we impute all.'[12]

2. *Man's Benefits Conferred*

After the definitions and comparisons of man's spiritual goods and the implicit conclusions concerning simple perfections and transcendental qualities, one would naturally expect the explanation of the term *conferred (praestitis)* to favor the argument drawn from exemplarity. Surprisingly, St Bernard accentuates the more pedestrian dialectic of efficiency. He states simply that God is the *author* of dignity, knowledge, and virtue. Man's accepted benefits *(acceptis beneficiis)* and the goods not his own *(bonis non tuis)* in the nature of things have a source other than themselves. This principle is personified; it is named 'the author and giver of everything' *(auctor et dator omnium)*. This benefactor is the font of man's spiritual goods: author *(auctor)* of human dignity;[13] giver *(largitor)* of knowledge;[14] and the gift of virtue *(munus virtutis)* comes from the hand of the God of virtue *(de manu...Domini virtutum.)*.[15]

St Bernard at times appears to contradict his own basic statement when, for example, he admonishes man not to use the *given* as if it were *innate (uti datis tamquam innatis)*.[16] But his primary consideration of man's good in the spiritual order was built on the *innate*, but *participated* quality of these goods. In addition, St Bernard's genial attitude toward 'image' theory makes his language of efficiency even more enigmatic. This shift may have any number of causes. In the first place, the causality involved in exemplarity is very subtle and might even appear contrived. Secondly, St Bernard may have been suspicious of analogical usage that by abuse and with a certain noetic facility could, in fact, be used to prove too much. Or it may be that St Bernard in this context had an ambivalent view of an argument built on analogy: could the *dissimilarity* be sufficiently guarded in an area where *similarity* was so strongly emphasized?

However this may be, St Bernard opts for a more gross, more vivid proof and in consequence a less deniable one. Starting from the effect, he seems to say, one can prove only the need of a *sufficient* cause and not an *exemplary* cause. But this leaves unexplained his treatment of the special kind of *effects* as revealed in dignity, knowledge and virtue as opposed to the *effects* as revealed in bread, sun, and air. A proof from efficiency will furnish St Bernard with an incontrovertible basis for the distinction between creature and creator—a truth vulnerable indeed in the doctrines of participation, emanation, and exemplarism. St Bernard's argument here is simple: a thing compositely good is the necessary subject of some causal action; it has a *maker*. But on the strength of his treatment of spiritual goods, he might have said with equal cogency and superior logic that ontologically prior to the fact of efficiency and more fundamental than that fact stands the very

ground of comparison: participated perfection. In this argument
from exemplarity, participated perfection is related to an essential property. St Bernard accepts this. We see limited perfection and its essential note is *its having been caused.* But there
is a second aspect to the question. St Bernard here shys away
from that aspect. The prior and primary message of limited perfection is that there necessarily exists a *maximum* and *unlimited
perfection.* The cause here is a *sharer* not merely a maker *(parti-
ceps non auctor).*

The demonstration of essential loveableness and consequent
total response is better made when a kind of continuity is seen
between perfection and perfection. But the benefactor may reveal
in his gift a loving agent who also wins our affection. But there
is no real continuity here. For the benefactor is *totally other.*
In this case conferral is discontinuous.

3. *The Goods Manifested to the Human Mind*

Man's goods are *participant* (exemplarity); man's goods are
received (efficiency); and man's goods are known to be such and
hence reveal something beyond the goods themselves. We must now
discuss the question of this knowing. St Bernard directs his remarks to infidels--real or imagined--for the sake of dialogue.
These are defined as those from whom the truths of faith are hidden[17] and, he adds, 'those who do not know Christ.'[18] But the infidel does possess human **reason.**[19] And he can function in virtue
of his knowledge. Even impiety does not rob a man of his reason.[20]
This is a crucial point: if the infidel does not know Christ
he does not know himself *(scit tamen seipsum).*[21] And through the
self-knowledge and through the knowledge of his spiritual and material possessions he comes to an inescapable conclusion: 'he is
bound with his whole self to love him to whom he owes all that he
is.'[22] St Bernard's vocabulary on this point indicates that these
truths are not *per se notum,* but are known after a reasoning process. He speaks of '...the perceived goods of both body and soul.'[23]
And in another text he **clarifies** the sense of *perceived:* 'by the
gift of his intelligence man *knows for certain* that he has not these
goods of himself *(certissime comperit).*'[24] The verb *comperire* suggests the discovery of a thing without fear of error. To this is
added the superlative *certissime*--as if to allay any fear regarding
the truth of the apprehension, or perhaps to indicate something beyond apprehension.

The noetic complexity is, however, stated in St Bernard's résumé: *satagimus demonstrare.* The phrase indicates something stronger than 'try to show' or 'engaged in showing.' The words suggest an
argument both complex and laborious: *to take the trouble to show* or

to have one's hands full in showing. The appeal to human reason in
this text enshrines an invitation to think the matter through and
to resolve the matter in a judgement born of critically examined
and antecedent premises. At stake is an authentic and rigorous reasoning process. Even in skeletal form the text's *a posteriori* argument will allow one no invincible ignorance. St Bernard's rhetorical skills do no violence to the logical sequence of his thought,
granted the tack he has freely chosen.

In brief the argument is reduced to the following propositions:
1) Freedom, knowledge, and virtue are real goods; they are diverse,
   limited, and gradational.
2) Their limitation is a special kind of contraction. By nature and
   by concept these spiritual goods are limitless and yet they appear in a limited modality *de facto.*
3) The limitations of bread, sun, and air are radical restrictions.
   Their limitation is *intrinsic.*
4) The limitations of dignity, knowledge, and virtue are, on the
   other hand, *extrinsic.* And as limited realities sharing the
   transcendental qualities, they appear as indisputable facts; but
   they find their explanation in an equally indisputable conclusion:
   the *maximum* in any genus is the cause of all in that genus; *unity*
   is at the root of diversity; whatever *simple perfections (secun-
   dum quid simplex)* is found in anything by way of *participation*
   must be caused by a reality to which such perfection belongs *essentially.*
5) God is this *maximum,* this *unity,* this *essential perfection.* As
   the maximum, unique and essential good, he alone accounts for
   what is good and simultaneously *reveals* his loveableness--the
   cause of loving God is God himself--and *requires a response:*
   the mode of loving God is to love him beyond measure.

Summary

Seeing in man's spiritual, diverse, limited, and gradational
goods perfections totally different from the specific perfections
of man's bodily sustainers, St Bernard is led to see these perfections of the spirit in a special light. Their limitation gives
conclusive evidence of the *maximum.* But when St Bernard names this
maximum, the names are *author, giver, donator*--the language of efficiency. It is clear that the exemplarity necessarily, if second-
arily, includes efficiency. But it is equally clear that efficiency
does not include exemplarity at all. The notion of efficient cause
can be applied with equal force in the search for the origins of
sun, bread, air, dignity, knowledge, and virtue. But exemplarity
applies exclusively to the simple, participatory perfections of
dignity, knowledge, and virtue. And about these St Bernard shows

real concern. Nevertheless, in his argumentation the formal and explicit treatment is in the order of efficiency. Only in an implicit way does he treat of exemplarity. St Bernard asserts that the human mind without faith can attain to the truth that God must be loved because he is objectively most loveable. The process involves a journey from created participated perfections to uncreated and essential perfection. And the middle term of this process is causality--efficient under one aspect, but both efficient and exemplary under another.

Epilogue

There is a stark reality which plagues our human condition: ignorance of our *duty* to love is inexcusable, but the *act* of love is *difficult,* indeed *impossible*. This fact is universally experienced and it essentially cripples our capacity to love God without measure. But it is difficult, nay impossible, for anyone with the powers of free will to render wholly to God's will the things he once received from God, and not rather to twist them to his own will and retain them as his own.[25] The experience is undeniable. But its explanation baffles human reason. St Bernard returns to the conviction of faith: 'The faithful, on the other hand, *(contra quod)* know well how complete is their need of Jesus and him crucified.'[26]

Saint Mary's Monastery
New Ringgold, PA

NOTES

1. Dil II.2.6; SBOp 3:121.

2. Dil I.1.2; 119: 'Causa diligendi Deum, Deus est; modus, sine modo diligere.'

3. Dil II.2.12–13; 121: 'Deo tamen in promtu est ingratos confundere *super innumeris beneficiis* suis, humano nimium et *usui* praestitis, et *sensui manifestis*' (Italics are my own).

4. Dil II.2.12–13; 121: 'Praecipua dico...quia necessariora; sunt quippe corporis.'

5. Dil II.2.14–15: 'Quaerat enim homo eminentiora bona sua in ea parte sui, qua praeeminet sibi, hoc est anima...'

6. Dil II.2.15–16; 121.

7. Dil II.2.17–18; 121: '...qua eamdem in se dignitatem agnoscat, non a se tamen.'

8. Dil II.2.18–19; 121: '...virtutem, qua subine ipsum a quo est, et inquirat non segniter, et teneat fortiter, cum invenerit.'

9. Dil II.5.7–10; 123.

10. Dil II.5.10–13; 123: 'Liquet igitur et absque scientia dignitatem esse omnino inutilem et scientiam absque virtute damnabilem. Verum homo virtutis, cui nec damnosa scientia, nec infructuosa dignitas manet, clamat Deo et ingenue confitetur...'.

11. Dil II.3.6–7; 122: 'Veritas quippe Dominus est.'

12. Dil II.5.14–16; 123.

13. Dil II.6.25; 123.

14. Dil II.6.27; 123.

15. Dil II.6.1; 124.

16. Dil II.4.1–3; 123: 'Est quippe superbia et delictum maximum, uti datis tamquam innatis, et in acceptis beneficiis gloriam usurpare benefici.'

17. Dil II.2.6; 121: '...Quod si infidelis latent...'.

18. Dil II.6.18; 123: '...eos quoque qui Christum nesciunt.'

19. This text is a classical example of Ft Bernard's rhetorical use of terms in the service of deep psychological truth. The italics are my own. 'Fit igitur ut sese non agnoscendo *egregia nationis* munera creatura, *irrationabilium gregibus* incipiat aggregari...'. Dil II.4.13-14; 122.

20. Dil II.6.24-26; 123: 'Quis item vel impius putet alium eius, quae en anima splendet, humaniae dignitatis auctorem, praeter illum, qui en Genesi loquitur...'.

21. Dil II.6.3; 124: '...qui etsi nesciat Christum, scit tamen seipsum.'

22. Dil II.6.6-7; 124: '...quia ex toto se illum diligere debeat, cui totum se debere non ignorat.'

23. Dil II.6.19; 123.

24. Dil II.5.8-10; 123: '...dum de bonis, quae a se non esse ex scientiae dono certissime comperit, boni **Domini** gloriam servus impius captare sibi immo et raptare molitur.'

25. Dil II.6.7-10; 124: 'Verum id difficule, immo impossibile est ad Dei ex toto convertere voluntatem, et non magis ad propriam retorquere, eaque sibi tamquam propria retinere...'.

26. Dil III.7.12-13; 124.

THE MEANING OF THE MAUNDY ACCORDING TO SAINT BERNARD

HUGH McCAFFERY OCSO

It was Maundy Thursday in a year of the Lord since the final session of the Second Vatican Council. The solemn evening Mass was under way and, after the reading from the Gospel, the chief concelebrant, in an effort to highlight the ceremonial washing of feet, declared with all clarity and cheerfulness that St Bernard had considered the washing of feet to be a sacrament.

The preacher had no doubt about it. The holy abbot had expressly asserted that the washing of feet was an outward sign of inward grace instituted by Christ. There was no room for argument. There was room for a question: If the saint regarded the washing of feet as a sacrament for the washing-away of daily peccadilloes, why had he not recommended its frequent or even daily use?

The pity was that the preacher had not asked himself that question before deciding that St Bernard had so sacramental a view of the Maundy. As it was, our homilist, had he but adverted to it, was quite hoist with his own petard, or as vernacular more suited to contemporary chaos would put it, he was boosted with his own bomb; his 'proof' proved too much.

The irony was further compounded by the fact that our preacher was using a manualist yardstick and not adverting to the fact that the theology manuals were quite sure that St Bernard held the washing of feet to be a sacramental (a Church-instituted ceremony modelled on the sacraments proper)! Ridiculous, but they had a vested interest: they had to 'prove' that there were only seven sacraments.

We must give credit where credit is due: our homilist had not made the mistake of the manualists; he simply had the misfortune of having a manualist mentality when reading a very monastic theologian. He was hypnotized by the frequent appearance of 'sacramental' terms in St Bernard's sermon *In Cena Domini*. And no wonder, with real sacraments and roving commission 'sacraments' hobnobbing without specific names or numberplates all over the early twelfth century! It was no place for one versed only in the cold courtesies of classroom theology. No, one has to lay aside the Saul-like armour of the manualists and the scruples of post-tridentine 'orthodoxy' if one is to move surely in the more involved and inclusive theological world of the sweet singer of Clairvaux.[1]

The sermon *In Cena Domini* may not be Bernard at his most mellifluous but it lacks nothing of his subtle simplicity and unexpected humour. It has a single message: the meaning of the Maundy. All else, no matter how important in itself or its context, is at most only secondary

How far this sermon in its present shape represents the actual preaching by its author is questionable. But there can be no doubt as to the place of the Maundy either in St Bernard's chronology of the Last Supper or in the twelfth-century cistercian timetable for Thursday in Holy Week. Christ's washing of his disciples feet came after he had given the Eucharist.[2] The monastic community's High Mass on Holy Thursday--to the delighted displeasure of liturgical experts--took place immediately after Prime, the Maundy just before Compline.[3] As a result the washing of feet became not only the high point, but quite simply the point of Maundy Thursday, monastically speaking. And what did the Maundy point to? That, as a certain translation of the First Letter of John expresses it, is our subject. A text from the same Letter contains the solution to our query and quest.

In Cena Domini opens with a reminder that Holy Week is a provocation to repentance. Not only is the power of the 'sacraments' recalled during these days such as to split stony hearts, it also opens the sepulchres of sinners in confession. Note the word 'sacraments' and the word 'confession'; they will appear in one way or another again.

Not all these 'sacraments' are equally manifest. Some require closer scrutiny. Bernard purposes to deal with these 'closed sacraments' or, rather, because they are 'many' with some; with three to be exact. Mention of 'many' may be safely taken as meaning more than seven.[4]

Before discussing the three 'sacraments' of his choice, 'suited well enough to the liturgical season,' he offers both a definition and an illustration of 'sacrament.' He is showing himself a debtor both to those in the monastic tradition and to those among them 'infected', to whatever extent, with the, to them, exciting techniques of early scholasticism. 'A sacrament is said to be a sacred sign or sacred secret.' Doubtless the reader is expected to advert to the humour implicit in this close fellowship of 'sacred' and 'secret.'

This definition may not appear a very good one--though it is at least as good as that supplied by Abelard[5]--but even the 'manually' dextrous will accept that it settles our term of reference as far as *In Cena Domini* is concerned. Those willing to go beyond the manuals will welcome Bernard's terms because they are so similar to the phrase 'the sacrament and sacred and secret mystery' he uses elsewhere.[6]

So much and so little for the definition. Before we turn to the illustration, it is right and just and unto solution to glance at an explanation--a rather rare thing in the writings of Bernard, who was more intent on sharing experience than explaining an utterance[7]--of the word 'sign.' Signs, he notes, are extrovert, they signal away from themselves; they have 'designs' on something else.

This brings the discussion by a sort of inevitability to the illustration. 'Sacraments' he likens to the symbolic gesture of

investiture. The thing ceremonially bestowed might be worthless;
the right bestowed thereby could well be worthwhile and worth wile.
Our Lord did something similar when, before his Passion, he made a
gesture towards, he bestowed a certain 'investiture' on, his disciples. His purpose was 'that unseen grace be shown/given[8] by a seen
sign.'

You recall how much our Holy Thursday homilist made of this
kind of outward-sign-of-inward-grace formula. He would have been
less sure of his conclusion had he known the ways Bernard uses
visible-signs-of-invisible-grace phrases. The evident earnestness
and ardour of the brothers at Clairvaux was for him 'a visible sign
of the invisible grace' of the Holy Spirit.[9] Still more to our purpose is it when he writes that what the bishops did 'visibly' to
the walls of Clairvaux's church on the day of its dedication is
what Christ does 'invisibly' every day to the lives of the men living there.[10]

For the consolation of our homilist, we note that immediately
after his words about 'sacraments' being 'seen signs of unseen
grace' Bernard writes: 'All sacraments were instituted for this
purpose;'--that is, of being perceptible pointers to imperceptible
good influence--this is the purpose of the Eucharist, the purpose
of the washing of feet, the purpose, lastly, of baptism.' Here,
then, is the Maundy among the Sacraments! But what does that indicate? Saul among the prophets, the weeds amid the wheat, Christ
between two thieves; individuality can survive mere surroundings.

But the Maundy has not been 'saved' from the sacraments. The
investiture image comes in again. Just as the token given varied
depending on whether a canon, an abbot, or a bishop were being invested, so too 'different graces are conferred by different sacraments.' Having taken the Eucharist, the washing of feet, and baptism in that order, Bernard now takes them in this order: baptism,
Eucharist, and washing of feet.

'What is the grace with which we are invested by baptism? It
is the cleansing from sins. For who can make clean what was conceived from unclean seed save he who alone is clean?'[11] Not the
sort of text a manualist would use of baptism, but it does emphasize Christ's conferring of the sacrament, as Bernard's use of it
elsewhere goes to show.[12]

The wiping-out of original guilt leaves us still with the side-
effects of the Fall, unruly impulses that easily prove too much for
us. The Eucharist or, as Bernard expresses it, 'the Sacrament of
the Body and Blood of Christ,'[13] comes to our assistance, quietens
our passions, and prevents our full consent to grave sins.

Having risen so far from the pull of sin, we find it desirable
to rid ourselves completely of our daily and practically unavoidable
venial sins. Our current condition is described in the words, 'If
we say that we have no sin, we deceive ourselves and the truth is not

in us.'14 The words that immediately follow on this text prescribe our cure: 'But if we confess our sins, God is so faithful he forgives our sins and cleanses us from all wrongdoing.'15

The text from Job may have seemed strange when applied to baptism; this text from the first chapter of the First Letter of John seems even more so when applied to the washing of feet.16 'That we might have no doubt whatever about the forgiveness of our daily faults, we have the sacrament of it, the washing of feet.'17

Our homilist could easily argue that this 'we have' means having the Maundy ceremony. It could, but the supposition is scarcely a possibility. In sermons for the Purification and Palm Sunday Bernard refers expressly to the processions held on those days and the way they went; the only Maundy mentioned in *In Cena Domini* is the Maundy that Christ himself did.

> Would you know that that was done as a sacrament--*pro sacramento*--and not only as an example? Listen to what was said to Peter: "If I do not wash you, you shall have no part with me."18

A little further on we read:

> And how do we know that this washing [note the 'this'] is pertinent to the washing-away of sins, sins that are not deadly and which we cannot fully avoid before death? From the plain fact that he who offered hands and head was told, "He who is washed needs only to wash his feet."19 He is "washed" who has no grave sins, whose "head"--his intent--and "hands"--his deeds and deportment--are clean; the "feet," however--the affections--while we walk in this world's dust, cannot stay completely clean. No, one yields, at least for a while, and more than one ought, and variously, to complacency or comfort or curiosity: "we all offend in many ways."20

> Nevertheless, no one should make light of (*contemnat*) or think little [of these faults]. It is impossible to be saved with them; their washing-away is impossible except through Christ and by Christ....However, it is not necessary to be over-anxious about them; he will forgive (*ignoscet*) them easily, yes, gladly, provided we confess them (*agnoscamus*).21

Earlier in *In Cena Domini* when mentioning baptism, Bernard referred to the water used; when mentioning the Eucharist he writes of 'the power of the Sacrament.' When it comes to the Maundy, grace is, so to say, more personally provided 'through Christ and by Christ' *exclusively*. While still in the world of 'sacraments' the scene, with typical bernardine subtlety,[22] has shifted from the sacraments to 'the great sacrament of our religion,'[23] Christ our Lord. 'All that he said, whatever he did, all that he suffered, never doubt it, was of his own choice, full of sacraments, full of saving power.'[24] Applying this principle to the scene in Luke chapter ten, where our Lord visits Martha and Mary, the saint writes: 'What our Lord and Saviour deigned do visibly once and in one place at one time he does invisibly even now all over the world in the hearts of the elect.'[25]

If the interpretation of *In Cena Domini* presented here can be accepted, it is easy to see that St Bernard did not hold the Maundy to be a sacrament, and did not need to counsel frequent use of any rite and ceremony. He was merely reminding monks of their need of Christ and encouraging them to go cheerfully on their way, the 'apostolic' way of continual repentance and rejoicing;[26] to use, in other words that 'tool of good work' that the *Rule for Monks* offers in the words about confessing one's sins daily in prayer.[27] A manualist mentality was/is in no danger of understanding so monastic a message.

Mount Melleray Abbey
Cappoquin, Co. Waterford

NOTES

1. See St Bernard, Ep 189,4 and his use of 1 Sm 17:33; SBOp 8:14.

2. Palm 3.4; SBOp 5:54.

3. Consuetudines, 21, in Ph. Guignard, *Les Monuments primitifs de la Règle cistercienne* (Dijon, 1878) 112-113.

4. Cf. SC 85.1: 'multae sunt aversiones nostrae, multae et infinitae animae necessitates'--more than seven reasons; SBOp 2:307.

5. Abelard, *Introductio ad theologian* I. ii, and *Epitome theologiae christianae* I; PL 178:984, 1695: 'Sacramentum vero est visible signum invisibilis gratiae Dei.' Also in *Epitome* 28; PL 178:1738: 'Est autem sacramentum invisibilis gratiae visibilis species, vel sacrae rei signum, id est, alicujus secreti.'

6. OS 3.4; SBOp 5:353.

7. SC 16.1; SBOp 1:89: 'nec studium tam esse mihi ut exponam verba, quam ut imbuam corda.'

8. '*praestaretur*' can mean either.

9. Ded 4.4; SBOp 5:385.

10. Ded 1.4; SBOp 5:372. In this Ded 1 context, the holy abbot's linking of confession and washing is rather obvious; for frequent use of the maxim of whatever provenance, 'Omnia in confessione lavantur,' see Adv 4.6; V Nat 6.8; p Epi 1.4 (all SBOp 4); Pasc 2.10; OS 1.13 (SBOp 5); Div 40.2 (SBOp 6/1); Ep 113.4 (SBOp 7).

11. Jb 14:4.

12. OS 1.13 (SBOp 5:338-9), QH 9.3 (SBOp 4:437).

13. V HM 3 (SBOp 5:70).

14. 1 Jn 1:8.

15. 1 Jn 1:9 ('God' is not found in the Vulgate version). See *De poenitentia* 24; PL 17:997.

16. St Augustine associates Jn 13:10 and 1 Jn 1:8-9 in his *In Joannis Evangelium* 56.4 (PL 35:1789), where, as in *In Cena Domini*, the 'Dimitte nobis' of the Lord's Prayer comes in.

17. V HM 4; SBOp 5:71.

18. Jn 13:8.

19. Jn 13:10.

20. Jm 3:2.

21. V HM 4-5; SBOp 5:40-2. With St Bernard's language here, compare St Augustine, *In Epistolam Joannis* I.6 (PL 35:1982): 'Sed ista levia quae dicimus, noli contemnere....Vis ut ille ignoscat? Tu agnosce....'

22. See Gilson's gentle gripe (too bad to be a thomist when reading Bernard!) in *The Mystical Theology of St Bernard* (translated A.H.C. Downes, London, 1940) p. 42.

23. 1 Tm 3:16, used in reference to the Incarnate Lord in, for example, St Bernard's V Nat 3.10; Circ 2.1 (SBOp 4); Pasc 1.12 (SBOp 5); SC 53.8 (SBOp 2); Ep 190: De erroribus Abaelardi VII.17 (SBOp 8).

24. Asc 4.2; SBOp 5:139.

25. Asspt 5.1; SBOp 5:250. Compare SC 6.7; SBOp 1:29.

26. Cf. 2 Cor 6:10, applied to monks in St Bernard's JB 7; SBOp 5:181.

27. RB 4.58.

THE WORKS OF BERNARD OF CLAIRVAUX

IN ENGLISH TRANSLATION

Cistercian Publications, in its Cistercian Fathers Series, brings into modern English translation the complete works of Saint Bernard. Translations are made from the critical Latin edition prepared by Jean Leclercq and H. M. Rochais, and published under the sponsorship of the Order of Cistercians by Editiones Cistercienses, Rome.

Now Available

CF 1   *Treatises I (Apologia* to Abbot William; On Precept and Dispensation; Prologue to the Cistercian Antiphonary; The Office of St Victor)

CF 4   *Sermons on the Song of Songs, Volume One*

CF 7   *Sermons on the Song of Songs, Volume Two*

CF 10   *The Life and Death of Saint Malachy the Irishman*

CF 13   *Treatises II* (The Steps of Humility and Pride; On Loving God)

CF 18   *Magnificat: Homilies in Praise of the Blessed Virgin Mary*

CF 19   *Treatises III* (In Praise of the New Knighthood; On Grace and Free Choice)

CF 31   *Sermons on the Song of Songs, Volume Three*

CF 37   *Five Books on Consideration: Advice to a Pope*

CF 40   *Sermons on the Song of Songs, Volume Four*

Other works will appear as the Series continues. For information, write

Cistercian Publications
WMU Station
Kalamazoo, Michigan 49008